Treasure Wreck

Arthur T. Vanderbilt II

Treasure
Wreck

The Fortunes
and Fate of the
Pirate Ship *Whydah*

HOUGHTON MIFFLIN COMPANY

BOSTON 1986

Library of Congress Cataloging in Publication Data

Vanderbilt, Arthur T., date.
Treasure wreck.

Bibliography: p.
Includes index.
1. Whidah (Ship)   2. Shipwrecks — Massachusetts —
Cape Cod.   I. Title.
G530.W5787V36   1986   974.4'92   86-212
ISBN 0-395-39975-0

Printed in the United States of America

Q 10 9 8 7 6 5 4 3 2 1

CONTENTS

MAPS AND ILLUSTRATIONS

(FOLLOWING PAGE 84)

Captain Cyprian Southack's treasure map. *By permission of the Houghton Library, Harvard University, Cambridge, Massachusetts*

Drawing of the *Whydah* by naval architect Steve Pope. *Copyright © 1985 Steve Pope*

"The Tracts of the Gallions," a 1720 map of the West Indies from Herman Moll's *Atlas Minor* (London, 1732). *Courtesy, Harvard College Library, Cambridge, Massachusetts*

"Kidd at Gardiner's Island" by Howard Pyle. *Courtesy, Fenn Galleries Ltd., Santa Fe, New Mexico*

An aerial view of the outer Cape. *Photo by Richard C. Kelsey, Chatham, Massachusetts*

Map of Cape Cod showing location of wrecks through 1903. *Courtesy of United States Engineer's Office, Newport, Rhode Island*

Thirty-foot waves smash the Cape's outer beach where *Whydah* foundered in 1717. *Photo by Richard C. Kelsey, Chatham, Massachusetts*

The sea cliffs of Wellfleet. It was off this beach that the *Whydah* hit the shoals. *Photo by author*

Pages from Captain Southack's journal. *Courtesy, Archives of the Commonwealth, Boston, Massachusetts*

A warning to treasure hunters in Captain Southack's hand. *Courtesy, Archives of the Commonwealth, Boston, Massachusetts*

Cotton Mather. Mezzotint engraving by Peter Pelham, 1727. *Courtesy, American Antiquarian Society, Worcester, Massachusetts*

Reproduction of title page of Cotton Mather's sermon, 1717. *Courtesy of the Massachusetts Historical Society, Boston, Massachusetts*

A view of the harbor and town of Boston in 1723. *From an engraving in the British Museum after a drawing by William Burgis*

Barry Clifford with reporters. *Photo by William F. Galvin*, Cape Cod Chronicle

Barry Clifford and Captain Richard Gray with coins from the *Whydah. Copyright © 1985 Brent Peterson. From* Parade *magazine*

When I was very young, my grandfather told me the story of the pirate ship *Whydah*. For many summers thereafter, I walked Cape Cod's outer beach, looking not for smoothed pebbles or flawless shells, but for pieces of eight. On winter nights when the wind roared under the eaves like the surf booming along the coast, I dreamed of finding a doubloon gleaming in the wet sand, the first of a cache of coins the waves would wash about my feet.

After years of searching turned up not a trace of pirate treasure, I concluded that it had been a yarn. The story of young Captain Samuel Bellamy, of his year as a pirate on the Spanish Main, of the fabulous treasure he plundered, and of the loss of his ship *Whydah* in 1717, in a storm off Cape Cod, was, no doubt, a folktale.

Much later, I happened upon a reference to the wreck of the *Whydah* that led me to another source and then another, until I was examining early eighteenth century documents from maritime libraries, archives, and old bookstores. Here was a contemporary newspaper account of how the *Whydah* capsized off the Cape! And here letters from Captain Cyprian Southack to the governor of the Province of Massachusetts Bay, describing his expedition to salvage the pirate gold a week after the wreck. Court records contained confessions of the few pirates who survived the great storm, as well as transcripts of the court proceedings against them. And sermons of the famous Cotton Mather recounted conversations he had had with the pirates as they were marched to the gallows.

The story of Captain Bellamy and the *Whydah* was indeed history, not legend. The exception is the tale of Maria, Bellamy's lover. But I would not be surprised if, someday, someone came across musty old records that prove there was a fifteen-year-old girl named Maria Hallett who lived on the outer Cape in 1716, and there met the young sailor with dreams of Spanish gold.

The story would have remained a chapter of pirate folklore, however, had not the *Whydah* itself been discovered right off the Cape Cod National Seashore in twenty feet of water and under ten feet of sand, still holding a fortune in pieces of eight and gold bars and layers of gold dust that ran through the sand "like chocolate through ripple ice cream." Here, not far from where so often I had walked the outer beach, was the only pirate ship that has ever been discovered.

Early in his expedition to locate the remains of the *Whydah*, treasure diver Barry Clifford remarked, "It is just too much fun not to let everyone in on it." So it is. This book, then, is the story of the voyage and the wreck of the pirate ship *Whydah*.

Treasure Wreck

CHAPTER ONE

"A Mighty Treasure"

THE SPANISH MAIN. November 1643. Half the Spanish treasure fleet, dispatched from Seville in August, had anchored for several weeks at Veracruz on the Gulf of Mexico before sailing on to islands of the Greater Antilles. The rest of the galleons had sailed for Nombre de Díos and Portobello on the Isthmus of Panama, then to Cartagena on the northern coast of South America, and later to coastal outposts of Central America.

At each of these ports along the Spanish Main, the riches of the New World had been gathered in anticipation of the arrival of the king's annual flotilla of treasure galleons. For weeks, mule trains bearing bags of gold bars from the mines of Nuevo Reino de Granada and silver ingots from Peru had made their way down steep mountain passes. The bags of gold and silver, and chests of precious stones, were loaded on the backs of Indians who struggled for days under their weight, traveling east along paths through endless jungles. Canoes packed to the gunwales with the treasure of two continents were poled down malignant rivers to the coast.

There, once a year, in these sweltering outposts along the coast, where not a breath of air stirred and the stagnant smell of pestilence lay over the harbors, "the spectator would remain thunderstruck," one Spaniard wrote, "at the streets crammed with chests of gold and silver."

For a hundred years, Spain had been draining riches from its personal treasure house of the New World. From the time of the *conquistadores*, who, with a few hundred men and a few dozen horses, had plundered the Aztecs of Mexico, the Carib of the West Indies, the Mayas of Yucatan, the Chibcha of Colombia, and the Incas of Peru — from that time Spain had claimed sovereignty over the islands of the Caribbean, over Mexico, Central America, and South America. And, with the sacking and pillaging of these ancient Indian civilizations and the mining of the wealth of their lands, the Spanish Empire had become the greatest power in the world.

During the next century, a million pounds of gold — bright gold nuggets and ingots, bullion and bars, heavy sacks of gold dust, golden religious medallions and gold plate — tons of bar silver and cast flat pigs of copper, coffers of pearls from the island of Margarita, topazes and emeralds, and chests of tobacco and indigo, all poured down to these squalid shanty ports, "things so marvelous," Cortes wrote eagerly to King Carlos I of Spain, "that they cannot be described in writing, nor can they be understood without seeing them."

Now, in the autumn of 1643, when the dark holds of the ships had swallowed so much of the gold and silver that the stately Spanish galleons were wallowing in the Caribbean swells, the annual fleet rendezvoused and the treasure was tallied. After taking on provisions, the sixteen galleons paraded out to sea, their flags and pennants flying, and began their slow voyage back to Spain.

The ships would beat their way against the currents and prevailing winds through the Straits of Florida and then thread a course through the uncharted *bajamar* — the shallow sea of the Spanish explorers between Florida and the Bahamas. This would be the most difficult part of the journey; the trade winds and equatorial currents that had all but swept them into the Caribbean on their voyage from Seville made it equally difficult to leave this so-called Spanish lake. Once the Bahamas were behind them, the ships would sail north with the trades and the Gulf Stream and near Bermuda catch the westerlies across the Atlantic to the Azores and Spain.

On November 15, 1643, as the treasure fleet tacked through the passage of shoals and coral reefs off the northeastern coast of Hispaniola, the shallow turquoise waters began to turn pewter gray. A cover of clouds hung as low as the hills of the tropical islands. All afternoon, the wind gusted up and heeled the heavy galleons bucking through the white-caps, strengthening as the fleet clawed its way on, butting back and forth through the channel.

After dark, a howling wind bore down upon the passage off a furious ocean. The treasure fleet had sailed into a hurricane.

With their towering gilded sterncastles and short keels, dangerously laden with treasure, the galleons pitched wildly in the storm. On board, Jesuit priests prayed to Our Lady of Carmen, the patroness of those who risked their lives at sea.

Gale winds blew out mountains of canvas. Masts cracked. Rudders splintered. Stumbling down the backs of forty-foot waves, plunging into the troughs, lifted again toward the heavens, the ships lost sight of each other in the black fury of the night.

By morning, the hurricane had blown north. As the sun bore through a rushing floor of clouds, the captain of one of the galleons, *Santísima Trinidad*, scanned the ocean to the horizon. He could see none of the sister ships. Each of the fifteen other galleons had sunk. For a hundred miles, wreckage floated on the waters of the Bahama Banks. And somewhere beneath these shallow waters lay millions of dollars' worth of gold and silver and jewels.

Eight years after the loss of the Spanish fleet, William Phips was born to a poor Maine couple with twenty-five other children. At an early age, William was apprenticed to a ship's carpenter and, after learning his trade, settled in Boston, where he found work in a shipyard. Later he became the captain of a sailing vessel. Around the harbor and in the taverns of the seaport, young Phips heard sailors talk of Spanish treasure galleons that had gone down in the West Indies. One wreck in particular sparked his imagination: the loss of the fleet of heavily laden Spanish galleons on November 15, 1643.

Phips was infected by gold fever. In 1683, at the age of thirty-two, after several fruitless years of trying to raise money to salvage the Spanish treasure, Phips left his wife and home and sailed for England to enlist the aid of King Charles II. Phips's presence and persuasiveness, perhaps bolstered by his belief in an astrologer's prophecy that he would find "a mighty treasure," was enough to convince the king to gamble that this rugged sailor might actually recover part of the huge lost hoard. King Charles gave Phips the use of a frigate of 160 tons burden, H.M.S. *Rose of Argier*, which Phips outfitted with diving bells and other equipment for the expedition and manned with a crew of ninety-five that he rounded up along the waterfront.

The *Rose* sailed from the Downs on September 5, 1683. It was immediately obvious that a more dangerous crew had never been assembled, even from the scum of London's quays. Sailors were stealing so much from provisions stored for the entire voyage that, before the ship started across the Atlantic, Phips had to anchor off the west coast of Ireland to replenish supplies. The private stores of wine, brandy, and cheese belonging to the king's two agents, who were sent on the voyage to protect the Crown's interests, were pilfered. Members of the crew smoked in the powder room and drank themselves into stupors, and, as noted in an account of the voyage kept by one of the king's agents, "For swearing and cursing I bless God I never heard the like before in all the ships as ever I have sailed in."

When the crew learned that the agents were complaining to Captain Phips, they threatened to maroon the two on a tiny Caribbean cay. Phips refused to discipline the men, telling the agents that the ringleaders were "some of the best men in the Ship and if I should punish them I am afraid that their consorts will mutiny."

Upon reaching Boston Harbor on October 27, the troubles that had been confined to the *Rose* on the high seas were brought ashore. Although the *Rose* was on a private enterprise and was therefore not a man-of-war, the crew fired shots across the bow of each vessel entering the harbor until that ship struck its colors; then the crew demanded from the captain of each ship the cost of the shot. The nights were

filled with drunken carousing and brawling on the streets
and in the taverns of Boston. Before the *Rose* finally weighed
anchor on January 15, 1684, for its voyage to the West Indies,
Captain Phips had been summoned to court more than once
because of fights started by his men.

On the Bahama Banks, days and weeks went by without
spotting anything like "a Rock wch ... apeeres Like a boate
Keele up," which was said to mark the location of the
wrecks. The crew rebelled, demanding that Phips join them
on a pirate cruise around the Spanish Main. Phips, who was
a giant of a man, rushed at the sailors, knocking them down
left and right with his bare fists, "like another Shangar or
Sampson," and quickly quelled the mutiny.

Within a week, however, the crew, ashore on an island,
plotted to take over the *Rose* and maroon Phips. The captain,
who was aboard the ship when he was warned of the mutiny
by one of the few loyal sailors, aimed the ship's cannon at
the men on shore, threatening to blow them to pieces. "Stand
off, ye Wretches, at your Peril," he shouted, as he prepared
the ship to sail, calling out that he would leave them to die
on the island as they had planned to leave him. The muti-
neers fell to their knees on the beach and begged for his
mercy. Not about to test his luck a third time, Phips dismissed every sailor at the closest port and assembled a fresh
group of men to join him on the treasure hunt.

Continuing his search around Puerto Plata off the northeastern coast of Hispaniola until his provisions and patience
were depleted, Captain Phips returned to England in the
fall of 1685.

King Charles had died, but Phips, again exhibiting what
must have been extraordinary self-confidence, secured the
support of the second Duke of Albemarle, who in turn

enlisted the assistance of a number of other noblemen. He was outfitted with two new ships, the *James and Mary* of 200 tons burden and armed with twenty-two guns, and the *Henry*, a small frigate of fifty tons. On July 18, 1686, Phips and his royal backers obtained from the Crown a warrant to "all such wrecks as shall bee by him or them found in the Seas to the Windward of the North side of Hispaniola" with the right to retain "all such Riches, whether Gold, Silver or Bullion or of what other kinds soever, as shall be found therein," except for one tenth to be reserved for the Crown.

By January of 1687, Captain Phips's divers were searching the shallow waters around Puerto Plata near the Bahama Banks, but without finding any evidence of the lost galleons.

Captain Phips sent out an expedition of two crew members and three divers to the Banks on January 17 with orders "to goe on the bank and make a search for the wreck" if they could "gett a slatch of faire weather."

The crew returned on February 7, dejected, discouraged. The divers met with Phips in his cabin to present their report. They had searched the Banks as thoroughly as possible, they assured him, until one evening when their boat was "amongst a parcell of boylers [rocks that were washed by the waves so that the water seemed to boil] they knew not off where; they were forced to Anchor all night & by Gods blessing it being very small breese of wind all night in ye morning they gott Cleare of them."

Phips was so disheartened by the report that he told the men he would prepare his ships to sail the next day to Jamaica.

At this point, one of the sailors slipped a large bar of silver onto the table.

Phips at last saw it.

"Why? What is this? Whence comes this?" he asked.

The sorrowful countenances of the crew suddenly changed. This was *treasure*, they cried out. They had found the wreck!

"Then thanks be to God!" Phips exclaimed. "We are made!"

The ecstatic crew now told the captain how the boat had searched the north side of the Banks, and then the south side, finally coming to anchor a mile and a half south of the Banks. They set off in a canoe to explore among the "boylers." On the trip back to the boat at the end of the day, one of the men saw through the shallow crystal waters a violet-hued sea feather. A diver jumped overboard to fetch it, thinking that Captain Phips might enjoy seeing this beautiful coral formation. The diver quickly surfaced without the sea feather. There, in nine fathoms of water, were scattered great cannon and other unusually shaped, coral-encrusted objects. One of the fifteen Spanish galleons had been found.

Within three days, the divers had brought up large casts of silver, three thousand pieces of eight, and a great quantity of plate silver.

The discoveries were first counted in individual "peeces of Eight." As the treasure trove was mined, the bullion and coins began to be recorded by weight. One day, for example, "baggs of Coyne Money Weighing 1139 lbs" were brought aboard the *James and Mary*.

Phips and his crew scoured the wreck of the Spanish galleon for six weeks, stopping only to let a storm pass and to observe the Sabbath. Day after day, the divers brought up from the bullion room of the wreck seemingly unending loads of silver in the shapes of pigs, sows, and bars, bags and chests of pieces of eight, plate silver, gold chains, and jewels, all encrusted with coral from nearly forty-five years in the sea. Other members of the crew combed the waters with long-handled rakes, finding coins that lay scattered among the galleon's ballast. The wealth from the sea was astonishing. Even "a bad day's work," caused by sickness of the divers, resulted in the recovery of 3931 dollars and 1500 half dollars.

Fearing an attack by a French privateer that had been spotted standing off the harbor at Puerto Plata and concerned about the coming of "fresh gales" with "many Tornadoes and great swelling seas" in which they could lose all their treasure just as the Spanish galleons had, Phips left the wreck and sailed for England on May 2, 1687.

On June 6 he arrived in the Downs to a hero's welcome "with such Treasure as to the Honour as well as Profit of the Nation no Ship ever perform'd the like." The *James and Mary* was put under heavy guard "to secure the same against any foul play that may otherwise happen to it," and the Comptroller of the Mint was summoned to weigh the salvage, "being wett, sandy dirty and rusty." The comptroller certified it to consist of "37,556 lbs 4 oz of bars and cakes of silver, and 347 lbs of plate; and of gold 25 lbs; 7 oz 9 dwt." The New England individualist had brought back to London a mighty treasure indeed.

Captain William Phips was summoned to Windsor by King James II, who knighted him on June 28, 1687, "in consideration of his Loyalty, and good services in a Late Expedition," and named him Provost Marshal General of New England.

Sir William Phips returned to Boston a knight, a hero, and a wealthy man. He lived with his wife in a "fair brick

house" at the corner of Salem and Charter Streets in Boston
and soon was appointed the first royal governor of Massachusetts.

The Phips treasure created a sensation. In the taverns and
inns of London and New England for years to come, there
was talk of his unfaltering conviction that he would find
the galleons, of his perseverance, and the sheer quantity of
gold and silver he recovered. And, for generations, the tales
of his remarkable expedition would lure many other adventurers to the Spanish West Indies in search of ghost galleons
still at the bottom of the sea.

CHAPTER TWO

"Upon the Account"

I f william phips could do it, a young Englishman reasoned several decades later, he, Samuel Bellamy, could do it too. Like most pirates, Captain Samuel Bellamy is a historical phantom, a man who suddenly appears with no past, and just as suddenly disappears into the sea mists.

Young Samuel Bellamy — Black Bellamy, as he was called because of his jet black hair and swarthy good looks — came from the West Country of England, that rugged seacoast of Cornwall and Plymouth known for its seafarers, where families of the same name still live.

Each year, West Country fishing boats brought many poor seamen to Newfoundland to fish, under contracts providing that they had to pay for passage home at the end of the season. The masters charged so much for food, clothing, and provisions that most fishermen found themselves bound for the next fishing season, and the next, and the next. Although there is no record of his early years, it is possible that this is how Samuel Bellamy found his way to the New World.

Or perhaps Bellamy was one of the many sailors serving on English privateers, sailing the seas to plunder French shipping, who suddenly was without work when England's war with France over the Spanish succession, which had lasted almost half a century, ended with the treaty signed at Utrecht in 1713.

Whether a fisherman or a sailor, Bellamy's life at sea had been a breakingly hard one, as it was for all seamen of the day. Conditions were harsh and dangerous; discipline severe, often unreasonable. Later, Bellamy would call those men who lived by society's rules, submitting to the leadership of others, "Cowardly whelps," "hen-hearted numskulls," snivelling Puppies," and "chuckle-headed Fools," and those in power, "a pack of crafty Rascals," "Scoundrels," and "Villains" who robbed the poor "under the cover of Law."

It was not surprising that an intelligent, disaffected sailor like Samuel Bellamy would be fascinated by the tales he heard of the fleet of ten Spanish galleons, laden with "specie and plate," that had recently sunk off the coast of Florida in the hurricane of July 30, 1715. Like Phips, he became obsessed with seeking his fortune by salvaging this sunken hoard, said to consist of 2290 chests of newly minted silver coins. He too would become wealthy and be knighted and live the life of a gentleman.

Early in 1716, Samuel Bellamy acquired an old sloop and set out to seek support for his expedition. On his way to the Caribbean, he moored his sloop in Eastham Harbor on outer Cape Cod, staying for a while at Higgins Tavern in the Southern Parish of Eastham. There the young seafarer met fifteen-year-old Maria Hallett.

Together, day after day, they wandered out past the village along cart paths through the scrub pines, across sandy moors of dusty miller and salt-spray rose, through silver-green beach grass to the bluffs overlooking the sea. As they lay on the sand on those sunny days, watching waves roll in to shore, Samuel Bellamy told Maria of the wrecks, of the treasure that would be his. He would return with his sloop's hold full of chests of rings and chains of gold, of uncut sapphires and emeralds, of rubies and diamonds set in gold crosses, and of flour bags full of doubloons and ducats, guineas, and pieces of eight. When he returned, he would take Maria to the Spanish Main and make her his princess of an island of the West Indies.

The surge of the surf during those days was a call to Samuel Bellamy to be on his way. From the bluff above the beach, Maria watched as his sloop sailed out the harbor through the inlet to the sea. She watched when she could no longer distinguish its shape as a ship, and long after it had become a part of the sea and sky.

Day after day, as the ocean sparkled in the summer sun and still later as the sound of autumn roared in the breakers, Maria returned to the bluffs to watch the sailing ships pass off the coast, waiting for Samuel Bellamy's treasure-laden sloop to return.

That winter, a disgrace to the God-fearing Halletts of Eastham, hidden in the barn of Elder John Knowles, Maria gave birth to Bellamy's child. The baby choked on a piece of straw and died. Maria was found, and the village selectmen put her in the Eastham jail to be tried for murder.

Time and again, captivated by the charm of the young girl,
her jailors let her escape. The sheriff didn't mind; all he had
to do to find her was to look out across the moors where she
would be walking on the bluffs. Mystified by her ability to
escape from jail at will, convinced she was a witch, the
townspeople drove her out of town.

Maria built a hut on the moors of the tablelands above the
beach, where, from her doorway, she could scan the sea.
There she continued her vigil, waiting for Samuel Bellamy's
return.

Sailing down the New England coast early in the spring of
1716, Bellamy had met forty-year-old Paulsgrave Williams,
a goldsmith living in Newport, whose father, a successful
merchant, had been the attorney general of Rhode Island.
Williams joined the treasure voyage to the Caribbean, and
the two adventurers became close friends.

After several weeks of diving off the eastern coast of
Florida near Vero Beach, amid other groups of divers sent
by the king of Spain, the governor of Bermuda, and the governor of Jamaica, as well as the divers of pirate captains
Benjamin Hornigold and Louis Lebous, the patience of
Bellamy's crew was as drained as the stores of supplies. No
bar silver had been raised; not a single Spanish coin had
been found.

The thought of returning to New England empty-handed
was intolerable. The idea of shipping out again as sailors was
unacceptable. The crew's desire for treasure, the same sort
of impatience that William Phips had combatted, was un-
relenting. In this paradise of azure seas and steady trade
winds, of narrow shipping passages, uninhabited islands,
and hidden cays and coves, the lure of piracy was irresistible.

Merchant vessels sailing the trade routes of the Spanish Main had to pass through the Straits of Florida, or Crooked Island Passage in the Bahamas, through Windward Passage between Cuba and Hispaniola, or Mona Passage between Hispaniola and Puerto Rico, and there, waiting for them, would be a swift pirate sloop. In those years, several hundred pirate ships haunted the Caribbean. "North and South America are infested with these rogues," wrote the governor of Bermuda in 1717. And the governor of Jamaica complained that "there is hardly a ship or vessel coming in or going out of this island that is not plundered." Now, too, Samuel Bellamy and Paulsgrave Williams decided to give up their treasure expedition and "go upon the account." They would try their luck as pirates on the high seas.

"In an honest service," pirate captain Bartholomew Roberts later would say, in words that must have reflected Samuel Bellamy's thoughts, "there is thin rations, low wages and hard labor; in this, plenty and satiety, pleasure and ease, liberty and power; and who would not balance creditor on this side, when all the hazard that is run for it, at worst, is only a sour look or two at choking. No, a merry life and a short one shall be my motto."

Undoubtedly, they were encouraged by Captain Benjamin Hornigold. Recognized as a founding father of piracy on the Spanish Main, old Captain Hornigold would brag most about the orphan from Bristol, England, who had found a berth on a merchantship, deserted in the Caribbean, worked his way to New Providence in the Bahamas, and joined Hornigold's crew. Edward Teach was his name.

Dressed in black, with a greasy black beard that hung to his waist, his chest crossed with a bandolier holding three brace of cocked pistols, with ten-pound cutlasses, additional pistols, and daggers hanging from his belt, slow-burning matches smoldering in his hair and beard and under his hat, Teach — Blackbeard, as he was called — seemed to merchant seamen, as he boarded their ships, the Devil himself.

Hornigold recognized the talents of this hulking, drunken, intimidating man, and in 1716 gave him command of one of his prize vessels. Teach soon split off on his own to terrorize the Caribbean and the eastern seaboard. It must have seemed to Captain Hornigold a good time to teach his trade to other beginners, so, in the spring of 1716, Samuel Bellamy, Paul Williams, and their diving crew joined the pirate band of Captain Hornigold, commander of the sloop *Mary Anne*, and Captain Louis Lebous, master of the sloop *Postillion*, who together worked the waters of the Caribbean. Captain Lebous's *Postillion* was manned chiefly with Frenchmen, while Captain Hornigold's crew consisted primarily of Englishmen. Each sloop was mounted with eight guns and had a crew of eighty to ninety men.

That spring, captains Hornigold and Lebous led their pirates on a cruise around the Spanish Main "to Portobello . . . then . . . for the Havana, and from thence to Cuba, where they met with a Pink, an English-man Master, and took out some Powder and Shot and some Men." In May 1716 they captured a ship "to the Leeward of the Havana" on a "voyage with Logwood to Holland." The pirates "kept the Ship about 8 or 10 Days and then having taken out of her what they thought proper delivered her back to some of the Men who belonged to her." They took "without any resistance" two Spanish brigantines off Cape Corrientes (near the southwestern point of Cuba) "laden with Cocoa from Maraca." The Spaniards "not coming up to the Pirates' demand about the ransome were put a-shoar and their Briganteens burn'd."

The pirates sailed on to the "Isle of Pines [off the south-western coast of Cuba], where meeting with 3 or 4 English Sloops empty, they made use of them in cleaning their own, and gave them back." From there "they sailed to Hispaniola in the latter end of May, where they tarried about 3 months."

The two pirate ships dropped anchor in a lonely bay, sheltered by reefs from the Atlantic rollers. It was here in this tropical paradise, in June 1716, that a dispute arose among the pirates. Captain Hornigold and some of the English pirates had refused to attack an English ship. The rest of the crew, "some being for one Nation and some for another," demanded that every merchant ship be taken.

A pirate crew elected its captain and could just as easily depose him. "They only permit him to be captain," a contemporary history of piracy reported, "on condition that they may be captain over him." The crew shared the ship and shared its treasure, and all major decisions were made by a show of hands. And so it was that the crew of the *Mary Anne* voted to pursue all ships on the high seas, regardless of nationality, and "Bellamy was chosen by a great Majority their Captain."

Captain Hornigold "departed with 26 hands in a prize Sloop, Bellamy having then on Board about 90 men." A captain whose ship was later seized by Captain Bellamy would report that "the greatest part of the said Pirates Crew are Natives of Great Britain and Ireland, the rest consisting of divers Nations and of 25 Negroes, taken out of a Guinea Ship." Paul Williams was elected Bellamy's quartermaster, the second in command, responsible for the crew of the *Mary Anne* and the division of plunder.

A pirate captain, as one contemporary pirate lord remarked, must be "a Man of Courage, and skill'd in Navigation, one, who by his Council and Bravery seems best able
to defend this Commonwealth, and ward us from Dangers
and Tempests of an instable Element, and the fatal Conse-
quences of Anarchy." Bellamy's character must have been
dominating and recklessly brave to win the support of a
band of seadogs only weeks after meeting them, and especially to have overthrown one of the very fathers of piracy.

The new pirate leader was led to the great cabin of the
Mary Anne where the quartermaster, speaking for the crew,
pledged their loyalty. Then, the quartermaster presented a
sword to the captain, saying, "This is the commission under
which you are to act; may you prove fortunate to yourself
and us."

There remained one more formality: Pirate crews were
governed by a code of laws developed over the years by the
buccaneers of the West Indies. Signed and sworn to by each
pirate before a cruise commenced, the articles of the code
established the rules of a voyage, and how the loot was to
be divided. The articles of the contemporary pirate crew of
Captain Bartholomew Roberts were probably similar to the
articles agreed upon when Samuel Bellamy became captain:

I. Every man shall have an equal vote in affairs of moment. He shall have an equal title to the fresh provisions or
strong liquors at any time seized, and shall use them at
pleasure unless a scarcity may make it necessary for the
common good that a retrenchment may be voted.

II. Every man shall be called fairly in turn by the list on
board of prizes. But if they defraud the company to the
value of even a Piece of Eight in plate, jewels or money,

they shall be marooned. If any man rob another he shall have his nose and ears slit, and be put ashore where he shall be sure to encounter hardships.

III. None shall game for money either with dice or cards.

IV. The lights and candles should be put out at eight at night, and if any of the crew desire to drink after that hour they shall sit upon the open deck without lights.

V. Each man shall keep his piece, cutlass and pistols at all times clean and ready for action.

VI. No boy or woman to be allowed amongst them. If any man shall be found seducing any of the latter sex and carrying her to sea in disguise he shall suffer death.

VII. He that shall desert the ship or his quarters in time of battle shall be punished by death or marooning.

VIII. None shall strike another on board the ship, but every man's quarrel shall be ended on shore by sword or pistol in this manner. At the word of command from the quartermaster, each man being previously placed back to back, shall turn and fire immediately. If any man do not, the quartermaster shall knock the piece out of his hand. If both miss their aim they shall take to their cutlasses, and he that draweth first blood shall be declared the victor.

IX. No man shall talk of breaking up their way of living till each has a share of 1,000 [pounds]. Every man who shall become a cripple or lose a limb in his service shall have 800 pieces of eight from the common stock and for lesser hurts proportionately.

X. The captain and the quartermaster shall each receive two shares of a prize, the master gunner and boatswain, one and one half shares, all other officers one and one quarter, and private gentlemen of fortune one share each.

XI. The musicians shall have rest on the Sabbath Day only by right. On all other days by favour only.

After Captain Bellamy's pirates signed the articles, the guns of the *Mary Anne* fired. Cheers of the crew echoed off the green hills above the anchorage, and sent bright flashes of tropical birds darting out of the forest.

From then on, "Bellamy and Lebous kept company together," sailing to the Windward from the Isle of Pines "to look for a ship of Force."

Each of the pirates of Captain Bellamy's crew, if ever captured, was ready to claim that he was a forced man, that he had been taken prisoner by this band of pirates and forced to join the crew. Some volunteers even requested that the pirates go through the motions of forcing them to join, so that if ever captured they would have witnesses and a defense.

With the exception of captives with special skills — such as surgeons, sailmakers, and carpenters — pirates rarely forced seamen into service, for there were always volunteers. Men like Thomas Baker, "by Trade a Taylor," who had left his home in Holland to go to sea at the age of twenty-nine, and Peter Hoof, a thirty-four-year-old Swede who had been a sailor for the last eighteen years, Simon Van Vorst, a young sailor from New York, and Hendrick Quintor, a twenty-five-year-old mariner from Amsterdam, all might claim that Captain Bellamy had told them they "must be easy" or he would put them "a-shoar on some Moroon Island," but their actions made it clear they were volunteers.

Crews comprised seamen who had had enough of the severe discipline on board merchant ships of the day, sailors who had been flogged with the tarred rope or cat-o'-nine-tails, who had been keel-hauled, towed from the stern of a ship, dunked from the yardarm, branded, or subjected to any of the other punishments meted out by sadistic officers. Other recruits came from the ranks of sailors tired of the back-breaking labor that was their lot. "Six days shalt thou labour as hard as thou art able," went an old sea saying, "the seventh, holy-stone the main deck and chip the chain cable."

Joining these discontented seamen were deserters from warships of the Royal Navy, runaway apprentices and indentured servants, escaped prisoners of war, debtors, adventurers, and the hundreds of privateers suddenly without a livelihood when England and France ceased hostilities in 1713. "Peace makes pirates," it was said. "War is no sooner ended," wrote the Bahamas collector for customs, "but the West Indies always swarms with pirates."

All were drawn by the same magic vision of easy riches, of a hold full of treasure from the gold and silver mines of South America, of coffers of precious stones and jewels, fabulous silks, elephant-trunk ivory, and spices, and chests of church plate, crowns and guineas, doubloons and silver eight reales, drawn by the lure of a life of freedom, of tropical paradises, and of great adventure.

In a day when sailors were little more than slaves, when they might earn a pound a month, pirate ships were returning to port with enough booty to reward each member of the crew with over a thousand pounds, a staggering sum equivalent to the income of the English gentry. In an age in which the lower classes had no way to rise above their circumstances, there was no shortage of men eager to join a pirate crew like Captain Bellamy's.

Without country, without home, were these bands of sea wolves. An outlaw, ever on the alert, Captain Bellamy sailed the Caribbean, unheard of for days, for weeks, lurking in the coastal shallows, patrolling the channels and straits, suddenly skimming along under a press of sail, his cannons roaring, swooping out of the dawn to plunder a cumbersome merchant ship, just as suddenly lost again among the endless isles along the Windwards.

So terrorized were sailors by the pirate tales they had heard, that their only reaction upon seeing a pinnace or sloop bearing down on them, flying the Jolly Roger, was to escape and, if captured, to surrender at once.

They had heard of the pirates who captured two East Indiamen in the Red Sea in 1695 and, annoyed by the talk of one of the captive captains, sewed his lips shut with a sail needle.

They had heard all about another captain and his crew who had been sewn up in a mainsail by pirates and flung overboard. Twenty bodies were found in the sail when later it washed up on shore.

They knew what had happened when the captain of a merchantship did not strike his colors when fired upon: the pirate crew, upon boarding the ship, "put a Rope about his Neck and hoisted him up and down several times to the Main-yard-arm, till he was almost dead."

Their dreams were haunted by scenes of pirates stuffing sailors' mouths full of oakum and then setting the oakum ablaze, pirates pulling out sailors' tongues, slicing off their ears, lopping off their heads, lashing them to the capstan and whipping them to death with a cat-o'-nine-tails, cutting out their hearts and making shipmates eat them, forcing their victims to walk the plank or throwing them directly into shark-infested waters, setting them adrift in small boats with no provisions, marooning them on tiny coral islands. "It is a common thing among privateers," one observer reported, "to cut a man in pieces, or tie a cord around his head and twist it with a stick until his eyes pop out."

The penny-pinching owners of the merchant ships manned them with as few sailors as possible. When pirates overtook a ship, firing a shot across its bow, with the pirate crew shouting war cries and swinging cutlasses through the air, the merchant seamen would come to and lower their flag, giving little thought to fighting to protect their employer's cargo. Their best hope was to give the pirates whatever they wanted, and pray that they would soon depart.

Because of this reputation, the work of pirates by the time Samuel Bellamy went upon the account had become very easy indeed: a chase, a shot of the cannon, and the ship and its cargo were theirs. There is no record that Captain Bellamy and his crew ever used force or violence to capture any of the scores of vessels they plundered.

At sunrise on November 9, 1716, Abijah Savage, commander of the sloop *Bonetta*, sailing from Jamaica to Antigua, spotted "two large Sloops betwixt the Islands of Saint Thomas and Saint Cruise [St. Croix]." The breezes were light, but it was soon clear that the two ships were pursuing *Bonetta*. The *Mary Anne*, commanded by Samuel Bellamy, and the *Postillion*, commanded by Louis Lebous, each "Hoisting a black flag at the Mast Head," immediately "fired a Canon Ball." This was enough to convince Captain Savage to strike his sails. The pirates didn't even have to board his ship; Captain Savage had his longboat lowered into the water and was rowed to the pirate ships.

The pirates helped themselves to what they wanted from the *Bonetta*, including "Several of their Cloaths, and other things particularly a Negro Man, and an Indian Boy belonging to Mr. Benjamin Wickham of this Island, who were then on Board." Captain Savage and his crew and passengers were held captive on the island of St. Croix, "where the pirates anchored for a great part of the time."

During the sixteen days he was held captive, Captain Savage watched as the pirates "took a French Ship, and Six Sail of Small Vessels, all of which (after taking from them what they thought convenient) they discharged."

Shortly before releasing him, Captain Bellamy told Captain Savage that what his pirates were looking for was a larger ship to engage in longer expeditions. They wanted "a Ship of Provisions, and to exchange their Sloop for a Ship, which if they could but get fit for their Turn they would go further believing they should be able to Conquer and make a Voyage."

Such enthusiasm of Captain Bellamy and his crew caught the imagination of one passenger aboard the *Bonetta*, John King, who decided to join the pirates. He was, as the captain of the *Bonetta* later testified, "so far from being forced or compelled by them . . . that he declared he would kill himself if he was restrained, and even threatened his Mother who was then on board as a Passenger."

Plying to the windward, the pirates reached Saba, a five-square-mile islet off the Virgin Islands, which rose straight up from the sea to its green mountain peaks in the clouds. Off Saba, "they Spy'd 2 Ships, which they chased and came up with." The larger ship, *Sultana*, was commanded by Captain Richards and the other by Captain Tosor, both bound for the Bay of Honduras. Having plundered the ships "and taken out some Young men [who] Cry and express their Grief upon their being compelled to go with Bellamy," they freed the rest, giving them back Tosor's ship and converting the *Sultana* into a man-of-war under the command of Captain Bellamy. Paul Williams was elected captain of the *Mary Anne*. Bellamy and Williams took their ships "to the Main to Water, from thence to Testegos, the Wind blowing very hard they went to St. Croix."

In September 1716, the *St. Michael*, a Bristol ship "laden with Provisions," had left Cork bound for Jamaica. On December 16, 1716, about twenty leagues off Saba, the ship was captured by Captain Bellamy and Captain Lebous. The *St. Michael's* crew was held captive by the pirates on the island of Blanco until January 9, 1717, when the ship was returned to its master, James Williams, after the pirates had plundered it. The pirates took on board the *Sultana* as new recruits fourteen men of the crew of *St. Michael*. One of these, Thomas Davis, a twenty-two-year-old Welsh boy who, at age seventeen, had gone to sea as a shipwright, was forced to join the pirates because "he was a Carpenter & a Single Man."

Captain James Williams entreated Bellamy to let Thomas Davis go, and Davis begged Bellamy for his freedom, crying that "he was undone by being detained among them." One of the pirates, hearing Davis lament his condition, said, "Damn him, He is a Presbyterian Dog, and Should fight for King James."

Davis begged the pirate captain to promise that he be set free with the next vessel attacked, a plea Davis continually renewed. At one point, Captain Bellamy asked Davis if he was willing to leave the ship. When the prisoner answered yes, Bellamy replied that if the crew consented, he would let Davis go. The captain then called a meeting of the pirates and asked "if they were willing to let Davis the Carpenter go." The crew, "by reason he was a Carpenter, expressed themselves in a Violent manner, saying, 'No, Damn him, they would first shoot him or whip him to Death at the Mast' " before they would let him go.

"To his great sorrow and grief" Davis remained a prisoner aboard Bellamy's ship. With another forced member of the crew, Thomas South, a thirty-year-old sailor from Lincoln-shire who had been his shipmate aboard the *St. Michael*, he plotted how they "would run away together," at the first opportunity. The pirates tried to make Thomas South a member of the crew, offering him arms, "but he told them He would not use any, for which he was much threatened."

At the island of Blanco, an islet among the Virgin Islands, east of St. John and not far from Dead Man's Chest, Bellamy and Williams parted company with Captain Louis Lebous. From Blanco, the two friends "Sail'd to the Spanish Main and water'd there and from thence to a Moroon Island called Testegos, where they fitted up a Ship and Sloop of their own." There, on the island, all the members of the pirate crew, which now consisted of 180 men, "were Sworn to be true and not to cheat the company to the value of a piece of Eight."

In late February or the beginning of March in the year 1717, Captain Bellamy and his crew pursued on the high seas for three days and nights "in the Windward Passage in the West Indies, a Free Trading Ship called the *Whido*, bound from His Majesty's Colony of Jamaica, to the Port of London, which Ship then was Owned and Navigated by His Majesty's Subjects of Great Britain, having her own Cargoe on board, and displaying English Colours."

Built as a merchant slaver, the handsome three-hundred-ton galley was named for the trading port of Whydah on the Gold Coast of West Africa. There, in the early eighteenth century, a thousand captives a month were taken by the Royal African Company for the slave trade to the New World. The pirates "thought they had lost her, but came up with her the third day." Other than firing two chase guns at the pirates, *Whydah*, "with 18 guns mounted and fifty men," offered no resistance to the pirate sloop flying the "large black Flag with a Death's Head and Bones a-cross" that had chased it all the way from the Windward Passage, between Cuba and Hispaniola, to Long Island, one of the Bahama Islands near Crooked Island Passage.

Captain Bellamy's pirates swarmed over the *Whydah*, taking hostage the ship's captain, Lawrence Prince, and his crew, and ransacking the hold. There, below deck, they discovered an astonishing cargo accumulated on a successful slaving voyage along the Guinea Coast, "consisting chiefly of Sugar, Indigo, Jesuits Bark [cinchona, from which quinine was made], Silver and Gold."

The *Sultana*, the *Mary Anne*, and the *Whydah* "came to an anchor at Long Island" in the Bahamas, where all the treasure the pirates had stored between decks on the *Sultana* was transferred to the *Whydah*. There, "Captain Prince was treated civily." He was given *Sultana* and "above Twenty Pounds in Silver and Gold to bear his charges," and allowed to load her "with as much of the best and finest goods as she could carry . . . Seven or eight of the Whido's crew joyned" the pirates; "the Boatswain and two more were forced, the rest being Volunteers."

Captain Bellamy could well afford to be generous with his captives. After less than a year upon the account, the *Whydah*'s hold was laden with treasure. "It was a common report in their Ship," one of the crew, John Brown, would later testify, "that they had about 20,000 pounds in Gold

and Silver." Pirate Thomas Baker confirmed that "they had
on Board 20000 or 30000 Pounds, and the Quarter Master
declared to the Company, that if any Man wanted Money he
might have it." And Peter Hoof, another member of the
crew, would later report that at the time "the money taken in
the Whido, which was reported to Amount to 20000 or 30000
Pounds, was counted over in the Cabin, and put up in bags,
Fifty Pounds to every Man's share, there being 180 Men on
Board. Their Money was kept in Chests between Decks
without any guard, but none was to take any without the
Quarter Master's leave."

Early in the morning off Long Island, the *Whydah* seemed
to float on its shadow above the pale green waters of Dead-
man's Cay. The crew had mounted an additional ten cannon
and swivel guns along the bulwarks, giving the *Whydah*
twenty-eight guns, a staggering number for a ship of a
hundred feet and three hundred tons burden. The men had
also stripped off the protective lead sheathing around the
hull to increase the ship's speed. Several tons of shot for her
cannon had been stored in the hold, along with a number of
water barrels, each weighing a ton, and heavy stones for
ballast.

With the tropic sun rising above the sea, Captain Bellamy
strode the quarterdeck of his new flagship, issuing orders as
the crew of young pirates scampered over the decks and up
into the rigging, hauling at the hundreds of hemp lines that
hoisted acres of white sails. *Whydah*, with a rush of power,
knifed the seas of Crooked Island Passage, riding the trade
winds toward the Greater Antilles.

With the *Whydah*, pirating was even easier than before.
When a cargo vessel spotted that ship bearing down on it,
with its twenty-eight cannon uncovered, surrender was im-

mediate. Captain Bellamy didn't even have to waste a shot across the bows.

Off Petit Goave on the southern coast of Hispaniola, the *Whydah* stopped an English ship laden with sugar and indigo, taking several of the crew and as much of the cargo as the pirates wanted, and then returning the ship to its captain. Several days later, the pirates captured the *Tanner,* bound from Hispaniola to Old France with a cargo of sugar. Below deck, the "Pirates found 5000 Livres," which they added to their sea chests between the decks of the *Whydah.* John Shuan, a twenty-four-year-old French sailor aboard the *Tanner* caught by the lure of the pirates' life, "declared himself to be a now a Pyrate, and went up and unrigged the Main top-mast by order of the pyrates."

Later in the year, Samuel Bellamy planned to go "a-pyrating" around the vast Indian Ocean, sail the Red Sea, anchor at the pirate haven of Madagascar, and capture some of the ships of the Dutch East India Company he had heard so much about, ships whose holds were said to be filled with huge cargoes of diamonds and rich silks, spices, rugs, and bar gold.

But first, what a sight it would be for Maria Hallett: the *Whydah* storming up the coast of Cape Cod, with every sail set and the lee rail awash.

CHAPTER THREE

"I Am a Free Prince"

THE MORE HE SAILED HER, the more Captain Bellamy came to love the *Whydah*. He grew accustomed to each change in the slatting of canvas and banging of the blocks, the creaking of the yards, the strum of the sails. He could almost sail his flagship with his eyes closed, feeling it heeling, pitching, skimming its way north through the Straits of Florida.

Like many of the brethren of the coast who cruised the emerald green shallows of the Caribbean during the winter, Captain Bellamy and Captain Williams steered north late in March, up the coast of the colonies toward New England.

The ships bound to and from England and the Leeward Islands would be off the coast of New England in the spring, seeking recruits and replenishing their supplies, trading cargoes of gold and amber, slaves, skins, and elephants' teeth for bolts of cloth and iron kettles. There the pirates could stalk the coasting vessels, sailing on to Cape Sable and Newfoundland for their own fresh supplies and recruits, later bartering the illicit goods they had accumulated between decks with eager merchants in Newport, Connecticut, and New York. "The pirates continue to rove on these seas," wrote the governor of the province of Massachusetts Bay in 1717, "and if a sufficient force is not sent to drive them off our trade must stop."

The *Whydah* and the sloop *Mary Anne* "steered away for the Capes of Virginia, being 180 men in company," following the Gulf Stream's oceanic current north, through its steep seas and sudden squalls of wind and rain.

For four days and three nights off the coast of Virginia, Captain Bellamy and Captain Williams battled a violent thunderstorm. In his *General History of the Robberies and Murders of the Most Notorious Pyrates*, published in 1724, Daniel Defoe describes this storm in such detail that it seems likely he had talked about it with a member of the crew of one of the two pirate ships:

"They were very near, as the psalmist expresses it, going quick down into hell; for the heavens beginning to lower, prognosticated a storm.

"At the first appearance of the sky being likely to be overcast, Bellamy took in all his small sails, and Williams double-reefed his mainsail, which was hardly done when a thunder shower overtook him with such violence that the *Whidah* was very near oversetting. They immediately put before the wind, for they had no other way of working, having only the goose wings of the foresail to scud with. Happy for them the wind was at W. by N. for had it been easterly, they must have infallibly perished upon the coast.

"The storm increased towards night, and not only put them by all sail, but obliged the *Whidah* to bring her yards aportland, and all they could do with tackles to the goose neck of the tiller, four men in the gun-room, and two at the wheel, was to keep her head to the sea, for had she once broached to, they must infallibly have foundered.

"The heavens, in the mean while, were covered with sheets of lightning, which the sea, by the agitation of the saline particles, seemed to imitate. The darkness of the night was such as the scripture says, as might be felt; the terrible hollow roaring of the winds, could be only equalled by the repeated, I may say, incessant claps of thunder, sufficient to strike a dread of the Supreme Being, who commands the sea and the winds, one would imagine in every heart; but among these wretches, the effect was different, for they endeavored by their blasphemies, oaths, and horrid imprecations, to drown the uproar of jarring elements. Bellamy swore he was sorry he could not run out his guns to return the salute, meaning the thunder, that he fancied the gods had got drunk over their tipple, and were gone together by the ears.

"They continued scudding all that night under their bare poles; the next morning the mainmast being sprung in the step, they were forced to cut it away, and at the same time, the mizen came by the board. These misfortunes made the ship ring with blasphemy, which was increased, when, by trying the pumps, they found the ship made a great deal of water; though by continually plying them, they kept it from gaining. The sloop, as well as the ship, was left to the mercy of the winds . . .

"The wind shifting round the compass, made so outrageous and short a sea, that they had little hopes of safety;

it broke upon the poop, drove in the taveril, and washed the two men away from the wheel, who were saved in the netting. The wind after four days and three nights abated its fury, and fixed in the North, Northeast point, hourly decreasing."

When the skies over the ocean cleared, the crew set up jury-masts. "All this while the *Whidah*'s Leak continued, and it was as much as the Lee-Pump could do to keep the water from gaining, tho' it was kept continually going." The ship's young carpenter, Thomas Davis, still the pirates' prisoner, discovered that the leak was caused by some oakum "spewing out of a seam" in the bow, a simple repair. Williams's sloop had suffered no damage other than "the loss of the mainsail, which the first flurry tore away from the boom."

The two ships hailed each other. Captains Bellamy and Williams agreed to head to Ocracoke Inlet on the Outer Banks off the coast of the Carolinas to check their ships. Southerly winds a day later forced them to revise plans and set their sails straight for New England. There they would rendezvous at Block Island off Rhode Island and visit Paulsgrave Williams's family, sail to Cape Cod to see Maria Hallett, and then on some deserted beach overhaul the ships.

The tension of battling the storm was broken. Off the southern coast of the colonies, it began to feel like spring. The crew "passed their time very jovially," and one of the pirates suggested that to celebrate their good fortune, they should put on a skit, "The Royal Pirate," a plan heartily endorsed by the rest of the crew, which already was celebrating the end of the storm with rounds of rum punch.

The quarterdeck was cleared. Roles were assigned. The treasure chests below deck were ransacked for "Thracian" togas and scarves, chains of gold, rich silks and brocades for costumes.

As the luffing canvas groaned and the long Atlantic swells rolled unceasingly past, with rapt attention the pirates watched the drama of Alexander the Great. One of the *Whydah*'s gunners in particular was drawn into the spirit of the play. As Alexander raised his arm to point to the heavens, the gunner looked up to see what he was pointing at, "creak'd his Neck," lost his balance, and fell against the bosun. When Alexander wept, the gunner began to cry. When Alexander captured the hero of the play, a pirate playing a pirate, he exclaimed, "know'st thou that Death attends thy Mighty Crimes, And thou shalt hang Tomorrow Morn betimes!" The gunner, convinced he was watching a real kangaroo court, raced to the stage to the hero's defense. "They were going to hang honest Jack Spinckes," he shouted to his comrades, "and if they suffered it, they should all be hanged one after another, but, by God, they should not hang him, for he'd clear the decks." "Taking a grenade with a lighted match," the gunner "set fire to the fuse and threw it among the actors." Other pirates in the audience who, like the gunner, had become swept up in the drama, rushed with drawn cutlasses to help save the hero pirate.

Before Captain Bellamy could call a halt to the melee, the pirate playing Alexander had lost his arm, the hero had broken his leg "with the bursting of the shell," and "Alexander the Great revenged the loss of his arm by the death of him who deprived him of the limb." Those in the audience who had rushed onto the stage were thrown into irons for a day with the gunner, and Captain Bellamy decreed that forever after "The Royal Pirate" never be enacted aboard the *Whydah*.

Several days after the storm, the *Whydah* lost sight of the sloop *Mary Anne*, but according to the agreement between the two captains, the *Whydah* cruised the coast off Virginia for ten days.

The *Whydah* was well positioned in the shipping lanes. On Sunday, April 7, 1717, five leagues east of Cape Charles off Virginia, at about eight o'clock in the morning, *Whydah* bore down upon the *Agnes*, a ship "bound from Barbados to Virginia laden with Rum, Sugar and Molasses & Sundry European Goods." Captain Bellamy "commanded the Master to come on Board." After the crew of the *Agnes* was aboard the *Whydah*, "the greatest part of the Cargo was plundered by the Pyrates, [and] carry'd on board their Ship."

The pirates that same day plundered three other merchant ships "of what Goods they thought fit" and took six of the crew of the ship *Lieth* "and two Men Servants, who voluntarily joyned with the Said Pyrates." They then put the crew of the *Agnes* and the *Ann* aboard the *Endeavor* and the *Lieth* and set them free, but kept as a prize the snow *Ann*, a one-hundred-ton transatlantic carrier that looked like a brigantine, with two masts and all sails square-rigged. Captain Bellamy ordered eighteen of his crew to man the snow along with ten sailors of the *Ann*'s crew who had joined the pirates.

The *Agnes* proved to be "so leaky that the Men refused to proceed farther" with her. On Tuesday evening, Bellamy directed Thomas Davis and another of the *Whydah*'s carpenters to board the *Agnes*, "who by his Order cut away the Masts and bored a hole in the bottom of the Vessel, and so destroyed her."

Captain Bellamy and his pirates had told the master of the *Agnes* that "they intended to Cruise for ten days off

Delaware Bay, and ten days more off Long Island, in Order
to intercept Some Vessels from Philadelphia and New York
bound with Provisions to the West Indies." Thereafter, the
Whydah would head for Green Island "to the Eastward of
Cape Sable" off the southern coast of Nova Scotia. There, on
a sheltered beach, they would careen the *Whydah*. The ship
would be run onto the beach on a high tide and, with a
block-and-tackle system attached to stout trees above the
beach, would be hauled on its side. Then, the many months'
growth of seaweed would be scraped off the hull, the barna-
cles burned off, and the holes made by the voracious teredos
plugged, with planks replaced and seams recaulked and
tarred. Finally, the entire hull would be coated with a mix-
ture of tar, tallow, and sulfur to inhibit further damage.

Fair winds brought the pirate ships and the prize snow
some forty leagues off the coast of Rhode Island, where
Captain Paul Williams and the forty men on his sloop captured a sloop out of Boston commanded by Captain Beer,
sailing with cargo to South Carolina. Williams had Captain
Beer rowed to the *Whydah* to meet Captain Bellamy.

While Captain Beer was on board the *Whydah*, his ship
was unloaded, and its cargo stowed away on Williams's ship
and aboard the flagship. Although Williams and Bellamy
wanted to return the sloop to Beer, their crews insisted that
his ship be sunk.

Captain Bellamy apologized to Captain Beer, explaining
that under the pirate code, he could not veto a general vote
of the crew.

Then, for several hours, Captain Bellamy urged the hostage captain to join his crew, expatiating on his philosophy
of piracy:

"Damned my Blessed," he said, his eyes sparkling like

black opals, "I am sorry they won't let you have your sloop again, for I scorn to do any one a Mischief, when it is not for my Advantage. Damn the sloop, we must sink her, and she might be of Use of you. Tho' damn ye, you are a sneaking Puppy, and so are all those who will submit to be governed by Laws which rich men have made for their own Security, for the cowardly whelps have not the Courage otherwise to defend what they get by their knavery; but damn ye altogether. Damn them for a pack of crafty Rascals, and you, who serve them, for a parcel of hen-hearted Numskulls. They vilify us, the Scoundrels do, when there is only this Difference: they rob the poor under the cover of Law, forsooth, and we plunder the Rich under the Protection of our own Courage. Had ye not better make One of us, than sneak after the Asses of those Villains for Employment?"

Captain Beer replied again and again that he could not break the laws of God and man to become a pirate.

"You are a devilish Conscience Rascal, damn ye," Captain Bellamy sneered. "I am a free Prince, and I have as much Authority to make War on the whole World, as he who has a hundred Sail of Ships at sea, and an Army of 100,000 Men in the Field; and this my Conscience tells me; but there is no arguing with such snivelling Puppies, who allow Superiors to kick them about deck at pleasure, and pin their faith upon a Pimp of a Parson, a Squab, who neither practices nor believes what he puts upon the chuckle-headed fools he preaches to."

Captain Williams had Captain Beer rowed ashore at Block Island. Beer would find passage to Rhode Island and reach his home in Newport by the first of May.

Captain Williams anchored off Block Island for several days to be with his mother, his sister, and his niece, regaling them with tales of his adventures on the high seas since he had left home.

The pirates of the *Whydah* and the prize snow sailed on, making "the best of their way for Cape Cod intending to clean their ship at Green Island" and "to get provisions."

On Wednesday, April 24, 1717, the pink *Mary Anne* of Dublin, Ireland, under the command of Captain Andrew Crumpstey, with a cargo of Madeira wine, sailed from Nantasket, bound for New York. As the *Mary Anne* sailed between the Nantucket Shoals, a stretch of shallow water some twenty-three miles east and forty miles south of the island of Nantucket, and Georges Bank, another band of shoal water ninety miles farther seaward, the crew on watch between four and six o'clock on Friday morning sighted two sails off the stern: sails of a large ship and a snow.

By nine-thirty that morning, the two ships, with the "Kings Ensign and Pendant flying," overtook the cumbersome cargo ship. Captain Samuel Bellamy ordered the *Mary Anne* to strike her colors. Lowering a longboat into the sea, seven crew members from the *Whydah* rowed to the *Mary Anne*.

Hearing the commotion, Alexander Mackconachy, the plump old sea cook of the *Mary Anne*, had climbed up from his galley and watched in horror from behind a mast as the seven pirates boarded the *Mary Anne*, five of them armed to the teeth with muskets, pistols "charged with Powder and Ball," and cutlasses.

Swinging a cutlass, one of the pirates, Thomas Baker, approached Captain Crumpstey and ordered him to climb into the longboat with all the ship's papers and with five of his crew, and to row to the *Whydah*. The pirates directed the mate, nineteen-year-old Thomas Fitzgerald, the cook, and crewman James Donavan to remain aboard.

Amidst the confusion of taking the ship, one of the unarmed men from the *Whydah*, Thomas South, hurriedly whispered to the mate of the *Mary Anne* that he was being held on the *Whydah* against his will and that he intended to escape as soon as the opportunity arose, words given credence by his behavior, which the pink's crew noted was "civil and peaceable."

Learning of the cargo stowed in the bulbous hull of the ninety-ton pink, four more pirates from the *Whydah*'s crew rowed over to the *Mary Anne* to bring some wine back to the flagship.

The pirates "hoisted the pinks boat off of the hatches and opened the hatches and then went into the hold." But because the anchor cable was coiled in the hatchway, "they found it difficult to come to the Wines in the hold, and so returned to their own Ship without any wine, Except five bottles of green wine which they found in the pinks cabbin and carried away, with some of the cloaths which belonged to the pinks Company."

The longboat was hauled aboard the *Whydah*. Captain Bellamy hailed the *Mary Anne* and ordered his seven crew members who had taken command to "Steer North-West and by North."

After an hour, Captain Bellamy again hailed his pirate crew and commanded the broad-beamed *Mary Anne*, which was lagging behind, to make haste. Out of earshot of the captain, twenty-five-year-old Jamaican-born John Brown swore that he would "carry Sail till she carry'd her Masts away."

In the meantime, several of the pirates were amusing themselves by teasing the old cook. Simon Van Vorst threatened Mackconachy, saying that "if he would not find Liquor he would break his Neck," and Thomas Baker said he would shoot the hapless old cook through the head because he steered to the windward of his course, telling him that he "would make no more to shoot him, than he would a Dog; and that he should never go on shoar to tell his Story."

Thomas Baker asked the mate of the *Mary Anne* who he thought the pirates were, quickly answering his own question by telling the hostages that Captain Bellamy and his crew had "Got a Commission from King George to act as privateers." Even Baker's comrade, Simon Van Vorst, had to laugh at that, saying "We will stretch it to the World's end."

All the while, the pirate crew was drinking "plentifully of the Wine on board the Pink." They ordered Fitzgerald "to reef the top-sail" and "Damn'd the Vessel and wished they had never seen her," for the *Mary Anne* was leaking badly and all hands, including the pirates, were "forced to Pump hard."

The ships continued sailing north by west until four o'clock in the afternoon, when the *Whydah*, the snow *Ann*, and the pink *Mary Anne* lay to, "it being very thick foggy weather." When the crew of the snow steered their ship alongside the stern of the *Whydah* and reported seeing land, Captain Bellamy ordered the ships to steer due north.

Later, as it began to get dark, Captain Bellamy paced the forecastle, watching the sails, watching the wind and the sea. He was becoming increasingly concerned about threading his way through the shoal waters off Cape Cod.

A sailor had been in the crow's nest all day, searching for the darker blue of the channels' deep water. Another spent the day taking repeated soundings. Now a fog was coming in. The purple-black sea was choppy with white-caps. It was no longer possible to pick out the channels.

Bellamy had taken on as a member of his crew John Julian, "an Indian born at Cape Codd," and a man named Lambeth as pilots to guide the ships past this coast. Even so, he was worried. He knew enough about the waters off the Cape from his stay at Eastham to understand just how treacherous they could be. Finding the channels through these shoals, even for John Julian and Lambeth, would be difficult enough in fair weather. And now, he was watching the clouds as they piled up along the horizon.

Early that evening, the sloop *Fisher*, bound to Boston from Virginia, "being laden with Tobacco, hides and other things," encountered "within a few leagues off Cape Codd," as one of its mariners recalled, a ship "of twenty eight guns called the *Wedaw*, which asson as they came near, haled us and Demanded from whence we came." Captain Bellamy called over to Captain Robert Ingols of the *Fisher*, "We are of the Sea," and asked if he "was Acquainted here." His luck was holding; Captain Ingols responded that he knew this coast "very well."

Captain Bellamy ordered Ingols and his mate to come aboard the *Whydah*. Four armed pirates boarded the *Fisher*. Bellamy instructed his men on the new prize sloop to follow his light.

As night fell, the *Whydah*, the snow *Ann*, the pink *Mary Anne*, and the *Fisher*, all "put out a Light a-Stern." The convoy began to beat its way up the most dangerous coast along the eastern seaboard.

CHAPTER FOUR

"Wind & Waves for Our Deliverance"

J UTTING THIRTY MILES into the ocean from the shores of "his Majesty's Province of the Massachusetts-Bay" lay the sandy peninsula of Cape Cod. The outer coast of the Cape, which faced the North Atlantic, was guarded by a Maginot line of shoals stretching far out to sea.

Submerged, shifting, and treacherous, a double line of these sandbars paralleled the Cape's outer beach from the tip of Monomoy off Chatham to Race Point at Province-town, lurking two to three fathoms beneath the surface of the water. The Nauset Indians of Cape Cod believed that the shoals stretched "beyond their knowledge" into the sea; in fact, they lay only half a mile to a mile and half off the coast.

Winter waves attacked the sea cliffs of this outer coast.

Ceaseless winds tore the tops off dunes, sweeping sand along the beach. Sand from the cliffs and dunes and beach was stolen by the sea and borne by the offshore currents until it was dropped in ridges out beyond the breakers. Here, the shoals formed and broke apart and formed again. Waves gathering strength over hundreds of miles of troubled sea were tripped by the shoals and crashed down upon them. Surf erupted into spray and seething white water foamed over the bars before the waves rolled on, their greatest force spent in breaching this first line of defense, on toward the shore.

Sailors learned that there was little hope if they were storm driven toward these shoals. When trapped on a bar, no ship could long withstand the pounding of surf. During the next two centuries, more than three thousand vessels from seaports all over the world foundered on the shoals and sank. Half the wrecks that occurred along the entire Atlantic and Gulf coastlines piled up on this lonely forty miles of outer beach — so many, it was said, that if all the skeletons were lined up, bow to stern, there would have been a wall of wreckage along the shore from Monomoy Point to Race Point. Here was the graveyard of the Atlantic.

"The annals of this voracious beach!" Henry David Thoreau exclaimed in the mid-nineteenth century. "Who would write them, unless it were a shipwrecked sailor? How many have seen it only in the midst of danger and distress, the last strip of earth which their mortal eyes behold. Think of the amount of suffering which a single strand has witnessed! The ancients would have represented it as a sea monster with open jaws, more terrible than Scylla and Charybdis."

That Friday evening, as the *Whydah* and its prizes sailed up the Cape's outer coast, the pirates who "had the government of the Pink" divided themselves into two watches, assigning the three hostage members of the *Mary Anne*'s crew to different watches.

When night fell, nineteen-year-old Thomas Fitzgerald, the mate of the *Mary Anne*, was at the helm.

With the night came wind, and with the wind, long, low, rolling thunder, a sudden rain squall, and lightning. By ten o'clock, "the weather grew so thick, it Lightned and rained hard, and was so very dark" that Fitzgerald had "lost sight of the Pirate Ship, Snow and Sloop."

The squall had struck with a roar. The *Mary Anne* lay over, forced down by the wind blasting off the sea, her lee rail awash. The pink lurched and plunged from crest to trough.

The *Boston News-Letter* of April 29–May 16, 1717, would later report that "the Pyrates being free with the Liquor that the captive had, got themselves Drunk and asleep, and the Captive master in the Night, thought it a fit opportunity to run her ashore on the back side of Eastham."

Such was not the case. Andrew Crumpstey, the master of the pink, was not even aboard the *Mary Anne*, having been taken to the *Whydah* that afternoon. And Fitzgerald seemed as shocked as the pirates when suddenly, above the gale winds, came that sound which haunted sailors: the roar of the surf under the lee bow.

"Being among the breakers," the crew "thought it most proper and necessary to weere [come about before the wind] the Pink," to force her back into deeper water. But "before we could trim the head sails we run ashoar."

It was "between ten and Eleven a Clock at night."

With a sickening plunge and shudder, the flat-bottomed *Mary Anne* had struck a bar in the seething shoal water. One of the pirates, Thomas Baker, quickly "cut down the Fore-mast & Mizen-mast of the pink" to reduce the pressure on the hull. In the howling northeast gale, sodden strips of sail and tattered rigging beat the sides of the stranded ship. The full force of the breakers began crashing against the *Mary Anne*.

Helpless, the seamen knew that it was just a matter of time — maybe an hour, maybe less — before the pink split apart. Yet to abandon ship, to try to swim to shore through the seas that thundered around them, would be suicidal.

"For God's sake let us go down into the Hould & Die together," one of the pirates shouted against the gale. The others followed. Stumbling down the ladder of the pitching ship, they pulled the hatch cover closed above them.

The hold was black, save for the flickering arc of light from a sea lantern swinging crazily on a beam. Empty bottles of wine and wreckage from the ransacking of the ship that afternoon rolled back and forth in the dirty bilge. The *Mary Anne* heaved and groaned as the seas pounded over her deck.

Huddled together in a corner of the hold, wet and cold, shivering, the pirates "in their Distress" begged Thomas Fitzgerald "to read to them the Common Prayer Book."

With the roar of the storm filling the hold, the young mate began to read in a slow, singsong voice, stumbling over many unfamiliar words in the holy book.

"The Lord is in his holy temple; let all the earth keep silence before him.

"The hour cometh, and now is, when the true worshippers shall worship the Father in spirit and in truth: for the Father seeketh such to worship him.

"Grace be unto you, and peace, from God our Father, and from the Lord Jesus Christ.

"Repent ye; for the Kingdom of heaven is at hand."

Clutching their bottles of Madeira wine, the pirates cried out in terror as a giant wave exploded over the ship and shook its timbers. The long, horrible, hissing undertow mingled with the wind, sounding as if it would suck the ship down to the bottom of the sea.

The candle in the ship's lantern sputtered, then steadied.

His voice quavering, Fitzgerald continued:

"Almighty and most merciful Father; We have erred, and strayed from thy ways like lost sheep. We have followed too much the devices and desires of our own hearts. We have offended against thy holy laws. We have left undone those things which we ought to have done; and we have done those things which we ought not to have done; and there is no health in us."

The cook glanced over at the band of ruffians trembling in the deep shadows of the hold. He wondered where they had come from and what crimes they had committed, what trail of destruction and death, of good ships captured and sunk, of misery and lawlessness, lay behind them. Surely it was God's will that they now must die. But why must he, Alexander Mackconachy, die, and Thomas Fitzgerald and James Donavan? Why must they, all good men, die too?

Drunk, scared, the pirates fell to their knees and tried to pray, repeating words after Fitzgerald spoke them. The mate continued on in the monotone of a poor reader, as outside, above the ship, the darkness burst again and again with thunder that sounded like cannons firing at the *Mary Anne.*

"Amen! Amen! Amen!" the pirates cried in response to Fitzgerald's reading. "Amen! Amen!"

Repeatedly, the storm and the sea joined forces to attack the pink. Down in the hold, the wildness of the night surrounding them, it seemed like the beginning or the end of a world.

"Deliver me from mine enemies O God," Fitzgerald continued, "defend me from them that rise up against me.

"O deliver me from the wicked doers, and save me from the blood-thirsty men."

He looked up from the *Book of Common Prayer* to the pirates, who were covering their eyes and ears with their hands, burying their heads between their knees.

With the wine and the lantern swaying above them and the mate's reading of words they did not understand, the pirates, one by one, began to fall into troubled sleep as the storm raged on.

That wretched night, as the pirates hid from the storm in the hold of the *Mary Anne,* the *Whydah* was beating its way north, ten miles up the coast, its sails double-reefed, its mainsail furled.

At the height of the storm, Captain Bellamy offered the captain of the snow his ship and his freedom if he would guide the *Whydah* safely to Cape Cod Harbor (now Provincetown Harbor) at the tip of the Cape. The captain of the snow, "suspecting that the pirate would not keep his promise, and that instead of clearing his ship, as was his pretence, his intentions were to plunder the inhabitants of

Provincetown," ran his snow straight toward shore, trusting that with its shallow draft he could head back out to sea before grounding, as the heavier pirate ship struck the outer bars.

If Captain Bellamy, windblown and stalwart, had been hurling "blasphemies, oaths, and horrid imprecations" to the heavens and readying his cannon to return the salute to the skies, as he had a month before, off the coast of Virginia, he stopped suddenly. Above the screaming wind that rolled her rails under, over the fury of the seas that tossed the *Whydah* about like driftwood, he heard ahead the booming of the surf along the coast of the Cape. *Whydah*, like the *Mary Anne*, had been driven too close to shore.

Bellamy's only thought must have been of the sea chests stored between decks, filled with thirty thousand pounds of gold and silver divided into bags, "fifty pounds to every Man's share," of the sacks of indigo and Jesuits' bark, the gold dust and jewels and ivory tusks, that remarkable treasure that he had worked for nearly a year to accumulate on the Spanish Main. The treasure must be saved.

Against the onslaught of rain blown horizontal by the gale and the sheets of spray and crests of waves lashing the decks, Captain Bellamy yelled for the anchors to be lowered.

"Drop anchor!" "Drop anchor!" "Anchor!" The order was given and repeated again and again until a crew of pirates wrestled with the capstan, lowering two anchors, each weighing a thousand pounds, with their huge flukes and rings big enough for a boy to climb through, and feeding out fathom after fathom of heavy iron chain, six thousand pounds of cable, that would hold the ship off from where the mad seas were breaking.

Dropping anchor while being driven toward the outer

bars off the Cape was the last-minute maneuver many captains would attempt in succeeding years after they had lost control of their ships, a last effort that failed almost as often as it was tried.

The anchor cable pulled taut, holding the ship off shore. But the *Whydah* at the end of the iron cable was no longer able to ride over the waves. Sails blew out with an explosive roar, the canvas thrashing as if wounded. Pirates hacked at the rigging with their cutlasses and knives to lower other sails. The three-hundred-ton *Whydah* stumbled into mountains of water that crashed against its bow and swept over its decks, each wave that it took threatening to swamp the galley. The anchor cable held, but at once the anchors began dragging, pulled by the *Whydah* as it was shoved by the tempest closer and closer to the shoal waters.

Captain Bellamy's only thought now was of saving himself and his crew. His feet planted as firmly on the wet deck as if he had grown there, he ordered a small sail set. "Cut the cables," he shouted. Axes swung, the heavy line attached to the iron cable parted, leaving the precious anchors at the bottom of the sea. Captain Bellamy spoke softly, encouragingly, to the *Whydah* as he fought to guide his ship out to deeper water.

It was no use. It was impossible to sail into the teeth of the gale. *Whydah*, defeated, could make no headway. As soon as the pirates cut the anchor cable, the *Whydah* "ran a-shoar," striking the shoals with a jolt, the great flagship trembling from stem to stern.

According to a sermon that was later preached by Cotton Mather, as the *Whydah* was breaking up and the crew realized that they must swim for their lives, the "Barbarous Wretches horribly Murdered all their Prisoners (whereof they had a great Number) aboard; lest they should appear as Witnesses against them. The doleful Cries heard unto the Shore, a little before they Sank; and the Bloody wounds found in the Bodies afterwards thrown ashore; were two great Confirmations of this Report."

"Alas!" Reverend Mather moralized, "how far the Wickedness of Men may carry them!"

Such nonsense could have been imagined only by the divine who had observed storms not at sea but from the study of his manse in Boston.

The "Great Hurricanoes" that had driven the *Mary Anne* and the *Whydah* toward the coast and forced the flagship to drag its massive anchors had heeled the *Whydah* drunkenly over to leeward and ripped canvas to flying shreds. Pirates and prisoners tumbled over the slanting, drenched decks, entangled in the fallen rigging, the snapped lines and torn sails. Water cascaded through gunports. The ship broached and the *Whydah*'s broadside was exposed. Waves swept men, screaming, overboard into the black water and wreckage. Heavy cannon ripped loose from their carriages and tore across the gun deck, smashing through the bulkheads. The slatting of the sails sounded like peals of thunder aboard the ship.

Even if the pirates had had any intention of killing their prisoners, they never could have carried out such a plan amid the madness of the storm.

Breaker after breaker climbed out of the ocean, thundering aboard. The *Whydah* was lifted, rocked, pounded farther onto the shoals. Pirates who climbed into the rigging to escape the seas were ripped from their perch by a mountainous wave that poured tons of black water over them. Within "a quarter of an hour after the Ship struck, the Main-mast was carried by the board." Pirate after pirate and prisoner after prisoner were torn from whatever rail or stanchion or line they clung to, and drowned beneath the thirty-foot waves. Decks were splintered. Spars cracked and tore away. Iron rods were bent as if of wax.

By morning, "she was beat to pieces."

The bodies of the pirates and prisoners that the waves brought ashore were indeed mutilated and beaten, but by the fury of the sea, not the wickedness of the pirates. More than a century and a half later, after the sinking of the steamship *Portland* in the record gale of November 26, 1898, with the drowning of all of its more than one hundred fifty passengers and crew, the marine reporting agent stationed at Highland Light in Truro reported that, for days, some of the surfmen whose duty it was to patrol the Cape's outer beach "were completely unnerved by their frequent trying experiences in dragging torn and sea-washed bodies from the surf. There were cases where some of the men of this service were made almost nervous wrecks by their almost nightly contact with the disfigured and unfortunate victims thrown up to their feet by the sea." The sea took its same toll on those swept from the *Whydah*.

This, Cotton Mather was sure, was "what the Compassion of our God has done for New-England, in the Inflictions of His Justice on an horrid Crew of PIRATES . . .

"The Good People of the Cape, saw a Marvellous Deliverance, in the Time of Tide, when these Monsters perished. Had it not been Just as it was, they had reach'd the Shore alive; and have made their way thro' the Blood of the Inhabitants, which Lived between Eastham, and the Hook of the Cape, where they would there have met with Vessels to have served them, in a Return to the Trade, which they had hitherto been upon. The Delivered People said, Blessed be the Lord, who hath not given us a Prey to their Teeth!"

Surely "Providence raised the Wind & Waves for our deliverance," concluded the advocate general of His Majesty's Province of Massachusetts-Bay.

"At break of Day" the next morning, Saturday, April 27, 1717, the first to awake in the hold of the *Mary Anne* ventured tentatively up the ship's ladder, pushing the hatch aside.

The storm had passed. The skies were clearing. The cover of clouds, breaking apart in the brisk wind, was awash with every color of dawn as the sun struggled to break out over the ocean.

To his amazement, the early-rising sailor "found the Shoar-Side of the Pink dry." The *Mary Anne* was right on the beach, having "run Ashoar opposite to Slutts-bush, so called, to the South-ward of Cape Cod."

The *Mary Anne* had been driven ashore on Pochet Island in the Southern Parish of Eastham, across from Slut's Bush, which was an overgrown piece of swampland in the middle of what was then the Isle of Nauset, and which had been given this intriguing name in 1626. That year, the *Sparrow Hawk* had been wrecked in this same area. One of the passengers, a Mr. Fells, had brought with him to the New World a woman he described as his maid and housekeeper, but who was suspected of being his mistress. When it became obvious that she was pregnant, the couple was ostracized by the rest of the ship's company and forced to camp out alone on this section of the Isle of Nauset, forever after called Slut's Bush.

The first of the *Mary Anne*'s crew to arise that morning

looked out over Slut's Bush to the mainland. Upon hearing the sailor's shouts of joy, the others scrambled up to the deck of the *Mary Anne*, rejoicing at their good fortune, and "all of them jumpt out upon an Island."

Far in the distance up the coast, the masts of the snow and the sloop *Fisher* could be "seen . . . in the Offen," riding safely at anchor in deep water. The great flagship *Whydah* was nowhere in sight. Soon the two ships slipped their cables, and, working their way northward up the Cape, oblivious to the shouts and cries of the pirates of the *Mary Anne*, disappeared.

The pink was "bilged on shoare, so that it [was] impossible to get her off." The pirates were stranded. Their comrades in the snow and the sloop had just sailed away. The *Whydah* was gone. But they were alive.

There on the beach, in the lee of the *Mary Anne*, out of the northeast wind that pushed the waves up on the shore and flattened the beach grass back on the dunes, "they tarryed till about Ten a Clock, and eat Sweetmeats and other things" taken from the chest that Hendrick Quintor and John Shuan had carried out from the hold of the *Mary Anne* and broken open. They washed down their breakfast with "the wines which came out of the Pink."

At first, the pirates "were in as bad a condition as before, being fearful," as Thomas Fitzgerald supposed, "lest they should be Apprehended." As they drank more of the Madeira wine, their fears disappeared. John Brown strutted up and down the desolate, windy beach, ordering the prisoners to address him as "Captain," and telling them that the other pirates "on Board were his Men." As they lay back in the sun after their breakfast, the pirates laid plans "to get to Boston and there Ship themselves as Sailors," with the hope of eventually meeting up with the rest of their comrades.

Around midmorning, the survivors spotted two men in a canoe paddling toward their island. John Cole and William Smith from the Southern Parish of Eastham had seen the wreck from the mainland, and had set out to explore.

When they landed and found the ten bedraggled men and learned how they had survived the tempest, they offered to paddle them to the mainland and take them to their homes, suggesting on each of the several trips to shore that the canoe be carefully ballasted with casks of Madeira wine.

At John Cole's house, the rescue was celebrated by breaking open the wine. It was only then that the old sea cook, Alexander Mackconachy, believing that his ordeal was finally over and that he was safe, stood up and cried that the seven were "Bellamy's men, so help me!"

Expressing no alarm, John Cole walked to a back room. There he ordered his young son to run to the home of the justice of the peace and tell him that there were pirates at his house.

John Cole returned to his guests and asked them "to tarry and refresh themselves." But now the pirates were wary. They looked, according to Cole, "very much dejected and cast down." The pirates asked him the way to Rhode Island, apparently hoping to find refuge there with Captain Paul Williams's family and friends, and then "made great haste from his house." The cook, who was quite pleased with himself, noted that "they looked very sorrowful, and made all imaginable speed in order to escape from the hands of Justice."

Justice Joseph Doane, the local justice of the peace and representative of the Great and General Court, upon learning that "there were some pirates journeying towards Rhode-Island," pursued them with a deputy sheriff and assistants.

The posse caught up with the pirates as they scattered out of Higgins Tavern in Eastham where they had stopped, a mile or two from Cole's home, to fortify themselves for their trip to Rhode Island. The pirates "talked in divers Languages" — Hendrick Quintor and Thomas Baker were Dutch, Peter Hoof was Swedish, John Shuan was French, John Brown was from Jamaica, Simon Van Vorst from New York, and Thomas South from England — but the justice realized that they all "were in a great hurry to go to Rhode Island." The pirates confessed to him that they "belonged to Capt. Bellamy Commander of the Ship *Whidoh*, and had taken the Pink *Mary Anne* in which they run on Shoar."

Justice Doane and his men tied the hands of the dejected pirates and marched them, along with the three men from the *Mary Anne*, who he assumed were also pirates, down King's Highway, which followed the old trail of the Nauset Indians along the dunes down the Cape, straight to Barnstable jail.

There were still two men abroad, however, who in the blackness and confusion of that stormy Friday night had been swept from the *Whydah* and miraculously cast onto shore alive: Thomas Davis, the twenty-two-year-old shipwright of the *St. Michael* who had been taken prisoner by Captain Bellamy in December of 1716, and John Julian, the Cape Cod Indian Bellamy had hired to help pilot the *Whydah* through the tricky shoals off the coast of the Cape.

How they survived the nightmare of the North Atlantic, how they found each other in the savage storm, remain mysteries.

Perhaps carried ashore on a spar, the two shipwrecked survivors at once struggled to scale the hundred-foot table-land bluffs, which the storm surf was attacking, and then crossed the rain-lashed moors. John Julian was in his own backyard, for then, in the darkness of a stormy midnight, they headed straight to the farm of Samuel Harding in Fresh Brook Village, a distance of two miles at the end of Solley's Hollow, near Duck Pond, in the present village of Wellfleet.

"At 5 morning," the two weary travelers of the night roused Harding and told him of the wreck. Harding at once understood. Without offering the two men food or rest or shelter, he had them help him hitch a horse to a wagon, and the three made their way in the gusty wind and rain back to the shore. There, they loaded the wagon with salvage and returned to the farmhouse, hiding the plunder deep in the recesses of Harding's weatherbeaten old barn, returning again and again to the beach before Saturday's sun rose over the troubled sea.

CHAPTER FIVE

"His Majesty's Loving Subjects"

It did not take long for news of the wreck of the *Whydah* to reach Boston. On Sunday, April 28, 1717, Colonel Buffet of Sandwich scribbled on a piece of paper everything he had heard about the wreck from Justice Doane and immediately sent a messenger, riding post, to Boston.

> We are informed [he wrote to the new governor] that there is a Pyrate Ship upon our Coast on the back of Cape Cod; who had taken one of our Vessels there, on whom he put on board seven of his Men, ordering them to steer after him: The Pyrates being free with the Liquor that his Captive had, got themselves Drunk and Asleep, and the Captive Master in the Night, thought it a fit opportunity to run her on shore on the back side of Eastham; which seven Men being examined by Justice Doane of Barnstable, the 27th of April past, whose Names are, Samuel Vanderson, Thomas

Beaker, Thomas South, Peter Hove, John Sho, John Brown, Hendrick Quinter, all Foreigners, Mariners or Seamen, confessed that on the 26th past, between Nantucket Shoals and St. George's Banks, they had taken a Ship called the *Mary Anne*, which was stranded on the Shore at Eastham, and that they belonged to a Ship call'd *Whido*, Man'd with about 130 Men, 28 Guns, under the Command of Capt. Samuel Bellamy, who had not any Commission from any Prince or Potentate; and that about a Fortnight before they had taken one Ship, and a Vessel call'd the Snow, 27 Men on board, and also two Ships on the high Seas. The seven Men are in Barnstable Gaol.

By the next day, Colonel Buffet had learned more about the wreck, and again dashed off a note to the governor, which a messenger carried to Boston that day.

The Pyrate Ship commanded by Capt. Samuel Bellamy, was Shipwreckt against the Table Land, on board whereof about 130 Men were drown'd and none saved except two Men, an English Man and an Indian that were cast on Shore. . . . A great many Men have been taken up Dead near the Place where the Ship was cast away.

When this news of the pirate wreck reached Boston, Samuel Shute, the new governor of the province of Massachusetts Bay, undoubtedly had visions and dreams of the remarkable good fortune of a former governor, Sir William Phips, who had recovered the fabulous treasure from the sunken Spanish galleon. What an accomplishment it would be for him to salvage a cargo of pirate gold right on the shores of Cape Cod! Governor Shute summoned the man he knew could do the job: fifty-five-year-old Captain Cyprian Southack.

Southack had first experienced military battle as a young

boy, when he assisted his father, a British naval lieutenant in the service of King Charles II, in the engagement of Southwold. He had sailed to Boston at the age of twenty-three with a commission from the Admiralty Board, had served ably on Sir William Phips's ill-fated expedition to Nova Scotia against the French in 1690, and in 1704 commanded the commonwealth's ship, *Province Galley*, in an expedition against the French and Indians in Maine and Nova Scotia. A skilled cartographer, Southack in 1694 presented to King William III his "Draught of New England, Newfoundland, Nova Scotia and the River of Canada" for which the king bestowed on him a gold chain. In subsequent years, he issued "A Draught of Boston Harbor," a map of the St. John River, a chart of the St. Lawrence River, and in 1717 a chart of the English plantations from the mouth of the Mississippi to the St. Lawrence. During this period, he had commanded a number of ships to protect the New England coast from piracy.

Governor Shute and Captain Southack acted quickly. By ten o'clock on Wednesday morning, May 1, 1717, less than five days after the wreck of the *Whydah* and less than three days after the governor learned of the wreck, Cyprian Southack was aboard "his Majesty's Sloop *Nathaniel*," as he wrote in his journal that evening in his cabin, the small sloop tacking through the choppy waters of Barnstable Bay (now Cape Cod Bay), "being bound on a Wreck cast ashoar on the backside of Cape Cod being by Information a Pirate Ship."

Scanning the horizon early the next morning, the low dunes of Cape Cod "Rose S.E. Distance 2 Leagues." The sloop "plyed to Windward" to round the tip of the Cape, but the seas were still running too high after the great storm to sail from the bay into the ocean. Knowing the coast well, Captain Southack understood that even under ordinary conditions "it is very dangerous to have [to moor] a Vessell on the Seaboard side," where the *Whydah* was wrecked.

"At 1 afternoon I came to Anchoar at Cape Cod Harbor," a harbor of twenty fathoms "wherein," as the Pilgrims described it, "a thousand sail of ships may safely ride." The curved sandy finger of Long Point off Provincetown, protecting the harbor on the west and south, had beckoned seafarers for centuries into one of the best anchorages on the Atlantic coast. Here, where sixteenth-century fishermen from the coast of Brittany and the Bay of Biscay knew they could ride out any storm, where the Pilgrims, after beating their way past the "dangerous shoals and roaring breakers" off the Cape's outer shore, "rode in safety" on reaching the New World, here in the harbor Captain Bellamy had tried so desperately to reach several days before as the *Whydah* was battered toward the coast, the sloop *Nathaniel* now swung easily at anchor.

Cyprian Southack lost no time that afternoon in sending his two deputies, Mr. Little and Mr. Cutler, by whaleboat to the neighboring village of Truro to get horses and ride across the dunes and moors to the wreck. By seven o'clock that evening, Little and Cutler had reached the ocean beach and dispersed a cluster of townfolk salvaging bits and pieces of wreckage. Lighting a bonfire of driftwood and broken planks, they established their watch.

Meanwhile, Southack that afternoon had "visseted" several of the ships in the harbor "and on board one of them found a Yung man boling [belonging] to the ship the Pirritt Took 26 April in South Channell, Saileing from Nantaskett the day before at 3 After noon." He learned of the recent cap-

tures the *Whydah* had made, and some of the details of the
wreck, all of which he would dutifully record in his journal
and report in his daily letters to Governor Shute.

The next day, Friday, May 3, at four o'clock in the morning, the hour at which he liked to begin his day, Cyprian
Southack climbed down a rope ladder into the old, shallow-
draft whaleboat he had commandeered on his arrival at
Cape Cod Harbor, and with the eight men whose assistance
he had enlisted in the name of His Excellency, Governor
Shute, cast off from the *Nathaniel*.

In the chill dark of early morning on Barnstable Bay, they
rowed the whaleboat down the coast, beaching at Truro.
There Southack strode across the moors to Captain Pain's
house, where he expected a horse to be waiting for his ride
across the Cape to the site of the wreck. His men would then
row the whaleboat farther down the coast and carry the
provisions across the Cape to the ocean, where the *Whydah*
lay wrecked.

These plans went awry. Perhaps Captain Pain, not expect-
ing his visitor from Boston before sunrise, was still asleep
when Captain Southack knocked at his door. In his journal
under the entry of May 3, 1717, Southack noted that there,
at Captain Pain's house, he "was very much affronted."

There would be many Cape Codders who rubbed Cyprian
Southack the wrong way, and whose misdeeds Southack immediately called to the governor's attention.

Most irritating to Southack was the delay in reaching the
wreck, for there were no horses to be found that morning in
Truro. The captain returned to the whaleboat, which his
crew rowed out to deeper water, steering south down along
the Cape.

As a cartographer familiar with the New England coast,

Southack recalled that an early English navigator, Captain Bartholomew Gosnold, who had explored the waters around Cape Cod in the spring of 1602, had referred to the outer forearm of the Cape as an island, perhaps the first record that there was a passage of some significance through Cape Cod.

A half mile north of the present border between the villages of Orleans and Eastham, through the lowlands below the rolling, cedar-covered hills of Eastham, across one of the narrow sections of the sandy peninsula, meandered Boatmeadow Creek, a tidal inlet from Barnstable Bay that worked its way east through meadows of salt hay. Another tidal estuary, Jeremiah's Gutter, choked with cordgrass and rushes, wandered away from Town Cove, west through these lowlands. Town Cove, in turn, led to Nauset Harbor and out to the Atlantic Ocean.

Only at the highest of tides had the headwaters of Boatmeadow Creek and Jeremiah's Gutter ever met, and it was at such times, Captain Southack remembered, that the early colonists had used this passage as a canal across the Cape.

Because of a rare alignment of sun and moon, that morning was the very height of the spring tides. Tidal waters surged into every inlet and cove and harbor along the coast. Time would be saved if the whaleboat could be navigated through this old passage across the Cape from Barnstable Bay to the Atlantic Ocean. Captain Southack decided to try.

With his long steering oar over the stern, the Captain guided the whaleboat in toward the shores of Barnstable Bay and up the mouth of Boatmeadow Creek, into the shallow inlet through the salt meadows, through the lowlands of the Cape.

The creek twisted and narrowed, the flooding tidal waters gurgling beneath the boat. When the oar blades hit the banks, the men stood up and poled the boat through the channel, pushing off from the banks of sedge and the muddy bottom.

Loaded with nine men and the salvaging "geer" from the *Nathaniel*, the whaleboat grounded. But once the men got out of the boat, the creek was still just deep enough to float it, and they hauled it with a length of line fastened to the bow.

Farther across the Cape, where Boatmeadow Creek met the flooded marshlands of Jeremiah's Gutter, the whaleboat grounded again and could no longer be dragged. Here the men lifted the boat with small ash bars slipped through pieces of leather fastened on each side, slowly portaging the whaleboat as they slipped on the eelgrass and sank in the soft ooze of the marsh. Soon the water deepened, and again they commenced poling and then rowing the whaleboat through the Gutter, finally reaching the open waters of Town Cove and Nauset Harbor.

Southack would later mark this long-vanished passage on his map of Cape Cod in the *New England Coasting Pilot:* "The Place where I came through with a Whale Boat being ordered by ye Govern[mt] to look after ye Pirate Ship Whido Bellame Command castaway ye 26 of April 1717."

Out past the crashing breakers at the inlet to the Atlantic, plunging through seas still churned by the storm of April 26, the whaleboat bucked up the coast to the scene of the "Pirritt Rack."

A driftwood bonfire fed by his deputies marked the spot. Holding the boat offshore, watching for a break in the waves,

Captain Southack, resting on his steering oar, suddenly cried "Now!" and the men bent to their oars. The whaleboat shot in on the back of a wave, in past the breakers, where Mr. Little and Mr. Cutler and Justice Doane helped the crew run the boat up the beach out of reach of the surf.

Fourteen hours after he had left the *Nathaniel* that morning, Captain Southack reached the beach where the *Whydah* had been wrecked. For fourteen hours, the fifty-five-year-old captain had helped steer, row, pole, drag, and carry the old whaleboat on its torturous trip. Now he was exhausted, covered with the mud of the marshes, and soaked from the spray that drenched the whaleboat as it fought its way out through the inlet to the sea.

As the beach and dunes were fading in the black of dusk, Captain Southack stood close to the bonfire that roared at the bottom of the tableland bluffs, its flames leaping in the gusts of wind. He stamped his feet, slowly turning to warm and dry himself.

Where was the wreck? the Captain asked his men. Mr. Cutler and Mr. Little pointed up and down the beach.

"The Pirate Wreck all to pices," Southack would record in his journal the next day, "North & South Distance from each over 4 miles." Caught in the heavy seas off the Cape's outer beach, the *Whydah* had "turned bottom up," and in the few days since the wreck, the timbers of the once proud flagship had been scattered up and down miles of beach.

Even more distressing was the report of what Justice Doane had encountered when he first reached the beach: "that there had been at least 200 men from Several places at 20 miles distance plundering the Pirate Wreck of what came ashoar." During the last five days, hundreds of Cape Codders from miles around had flocked to the scene with their horses and carts and stripped the beach of every bit of wreckage they could carry away.

There were no contemporary population statistics of the remote villages and farms of the outer Cape, but it is known that fifty years later, in 1765, the population of all of Cape Cod was scarcely ten thousand, and there were only a dozen houses in Provincetown. It was therefore remarkable that within twenty-four hours of the wreck of the *Whydah* on a desolate stretch of coast of the sparsely settled outer Cape, two hundred inhabitants had made their way to the beach, a clear indication that Cape Codders recognized the importance of this wreck above all others.

Early in the eighteenth century, colonial authorities had decreed that the finder of any part of a cargo from a wrecked vessel must report such finding to the town clerk, whose responsibility it was to salvage the wreckage and hold it for its owner. This was the law.

It was a law that was never obeyed. The Reverend Enoch Pratt, a historian of the village of Eastham, noted a century later that "The law requires that this should be done in all cases, yet it cannot be denied that it was frequently evaded, and the property found appropriated to private use, which has often been the case since."

To a Cape Codder, anything washed on their shores was a gift from the sea. Wrecking was their business as much as fishing and "whale fishing." In fact, in September 1854, when Ralph Waldo Emerson visited the Cape and stopped at Nauset Light on the bluffs high above the outer beach, "Collins, the keeper, told us he found obstinate resistance on Cape Cod to the project of building a lighthouse on this coast, as it would injure the wrecking business. He had to go to Boston, and obtain the strong recommendation of the Port Society."

Wrecking was in the blood of Cape Codders from birth. A young schoolmaster who in 1860 came to teach the sixteen students on Monomoy Point, a ten-mile finger of sand and dunes extending off the shores of Chatham beyond the beach where the *Whydah* was lost, was surprised to discover that his young pupils were wreckers. One of the students seated close by the eastern corner window, "where he could look up from his slate every fifteen minutes to scan the ocean horizon," took on the self-appointed task of keeping a lookout for wrecks. The schoolmaster noted that "the young gentlemen were quite orderly; and were duly amenable except on particular occasions, as, for instance, on news of 'wreck ashore,' when they were apt to leave pretty suddenly, forgetting even to say 'by'r leave.' "

The race was then on to the scene where "some passing craft hitched upon the outlying shoals." And, the schoolmaster reported, "if fates are propitious, out comes cotton and flour, and topmasts and yards are sent down, and running-rigging is straying on the breeze, and the stout ship is speedily stripped."

The wreck on the outer beach on March 4, 1927, of the schooner *Montclair,* bound from Halifax to New York with a cargo of laths, provides a vivid example of just how the wreckers worked on the *Whydah*. The *Montclair*, stranded in heavy seas on the bars off the coast, lost five of a seven-man crew. Quoting Kittredge's *Mooncussers of Cape Cod:*

> As soon as word reached town that a wreck was ashore, a migration started for the beach, Albert E. Snow among

them. Knowing that there might be something to bring home, he took his Ford beach wagon and picked up a friend or two on the way, one of them an artist who has made Orleans his headquarters for a number of years. . . . They left the car a little way beyond the lifesaving station and walked over to the beach. There lay the *Montclair* high enough to walk out to with hip rubber boots, the two halves of her hull a hundred yards or so apart, and, piled everywhere up and down the coast in chaotic confusion, millions of laths. Snow had his rubber boots, but the artist had come away without any; they therefore agreed that Snow should wade out to the wreck, collect what was to be had, and throw it ashore, where the artist should mount guard over it until they had a load for the beach wagon.

Snow climbed on board, where he found himself in the company of the best people in Orleans, twenty-five or thirty of them, young and old, who had come over to make a Roman holiday of it. The constable and his partner, who were house painters, were on hand, collecting enough rigging for use in their business to last them the rest of their lives. Others were stripping her spars preparatory to towing them round to Orleans as underpinning for floats. One man was at work removing the wheel; two others got the compass and most of the signal flags; the bell was carried out of town somehow, and so was the binnacle. At the rate at which things were vanishing, Snow saw that unless he jumped in with considerable vigor he would have had his trip for nothing. . . .

Snow and the artist loaded their trophies on the beach wagon, together with some goods that they were transporting for neighbors, and started back along the marshy route by which they had come. Halfway to the bridge they met another car, in which, as they soon discovered, was an angry man named Finnegan, a prohibition agent of some sort from Boston, who, as soon as he heard of the wreck, had started for Orleans to see how much truth there was in the rumor that she smelled of rum. Seeing the beach wagon loaded with stuff obviously from the wreck, he stopped his car and jumped out.

"Halt!" he cried. "Stop! That's piracy! That's plain robbery. Take all that property back to the ship!"

Snow explained that they were not robbers, but that their names appeared well up in the Orleans social register; everybody knew them and liked them, he continued, and as for turning round and taking these few souvenirs back to the wreck, it was out of the question: no car had ever turned round on that marsh without getting bogged. Let Mr. Finnegan drop round to the house on his return from the beach, and if he thought that they had behaved improperly, he could then at his leisure particularize; with which urbane remarks Snow went his way, nor has he seen Mr. Finnegan since.

Though less active since the end of the age of sail, Cape Cod wreckers have never become extinct. In 1974, for instance, some Barnstable residents stripped the sloop *Trull*, which had grounded on the flats of Sandy Neck, an incident that was reported and condemned in national boating magazines, with the wreckers referred to as the "thieves of Barnstable." And in August 1982, when the 73-foot New Bedford dragger *Venture I* stranded on the shoals outside Chatham Harbor, seven men on a Sunday worked for several hours to remove her 1000-pound bronze propeller, electronic equipment, and fittings, despite the threat of legal action by the ship's owner.

An old English prayer captured the ambivalence of Cape Codders' feelings about wrecks: "We pray Thee, O Lord, not that wrecks should happen, but that if any shall happen, Thou wilt guide them onto our shores for the benefit of the inhabitants."

If this was how Cape Codders reacted to ordinary wrecks, the frenzy that developed on April 27, 1717, when word spread that a pirate ship had wrecked on the outer beach must have been incredible. Now the villagers were not only looking for blocks and rigging and planking, but for gold and silver, ivory and indigo, jewels and gemstones.

Although disturbed by how completely the *Whydah* had broken up and by how thoroughly the wreckage washed ashore had been picked over, Captain Cyprian Southack was not discouraged.

Early on Saturday morning, May 4, 1717, he "imprest a whaleboat with six men to work on the wreck." The wind was from the south, "a Strong gale and rain," as he wrote in his journal. With his crew, he managed to row through the heavy surf out to the wreck, where he could "see her Anchor where She Struck first where I hope to get Something if any riches in her," but he reluctantly concluded that with the foul weather and "a great Sea . . . we can do nothing as yet."

Although the diving operations would have to be delayed a day until the weather cleared, Southack set his crew to gathering "pieces of cables and other things" from the wreck strewn along the beach, and to carting them the three and a half miles across the Cape to Billingsgate (Wellfleet Harbor on Barnstable Bay), where they would later be taken by ship to Boston.

As his men were gathering the wreckage, Southack

counted the bodies of the pirates lying up and down the beach. "There has come ashoar 54 white men and five negros out of the Pirate Wreck Dead."

Cold and wet, at two o'clock that afternoon, Captain Southack ordered the whaleboat and six men to return to Cape Cod Harbor, with orders to sail for Boston with his reports and letters to Governor Shute.

Galled by how little he had been able to accomplish, Cyprian Southack was now ready to teach the Cape Codders a lesson or two about respect for the law and for "His Excellency Samuel Shute Esq — Captain General and Governour in Chief in and over His Majesties Province of the Masachusotts Bay in New Eng. And Vice Admiral." Now it was time for the wreckers who had secreted what they had recovered in the root cellars beneath the trap doors in their kitchen floors, for those who had hidden treasure in their attics or in those tiny secret rooms behind the fireplace where the early settlers hid from Indians, who had locked it in their barns, buried it in their fields, now it was time to return the plunder to the governor's agent, Captain Cyprian Southack. Otherwise, as Southack warned in a stern notice he that day composed and copied and posted on church and meetinghouse doors, the inhabitants would be in the "utmost peril":

ADVERTISEMENT

Whereas there is lately Stranded on the back of Cape Cod a Pirate Ship & His Excellency the Governor hath Authorized and impower'd me the Subscriber, to discover & take care of S. Wreck & to Impress men & whatsoever Else necessary to discover & Secure what may be part of her, . . . with Orders to go into any house, Shop, Cellar, Warehouse, room or other place, & in case of resistance to break open any doors, Chests, trunks & other package there to Seize & from thence to bring away any of the goods, Merchandize, Effects belonging to S. Wreck, as also to Seize any of her men. And all his Majesty's officers and other his loving Subjects are Hereby Commanded to be aiding and assisting to me, my Deputy or Deputys In the due Execution of S. warrant or they will answer if Contrary at their utmost peril, These are therefore to notify all persons that have found or taken up any thing of S. Wreck on what was belonging to or taken out of S. Wreck vessell that they make discovery thereof & bring in the Same to me at Mr. Willm Browns In Eastham or where else I Shall order Or they will Answer the Same at their Utmost peril, and then all officers and other persons will give information of any thing of S. [Wreck] taken up by any person or Suspicion thereof, that they may be proceeded with and a Discovery made pursuant to my powers & Instructions.

Eastham May 4th 1717   Cyprian Southack

Cape Codders greeted the Advertisement with the same responses with which they greeted Cyprian Southack and Messrs. Little and Cutler when later they came knocking at their doors. "To what wreck was the good Captain referring?" some asked in astonishment. "Did his notice pertain to them?" they questioned. "No," others swore, "I haven't been down to that beach all year." Others laughed, welcoming him to try to find whatever part of the treasure he thought they might be hiding.

Captain Southack had of course first stopped at the farm of Samuel Harding. Harding exhibited the same Yankee ingenuity in dealing with Southack that had characterized his actions a week before when Thomas Davis and John Julian led him back to the wreck of the *Whydah*. He didn't deny that he had cargo from the wreck, but assured Southack that he was holding the salvage for Thomas Davis until after his trial in Boston; surely, he told the Captain, it would be an unpardonable breach of faith to renege on this commitment.

This Southack found absolutely infuriating. He lost no time in writing to Governor Shute and telling him exactly what he thought of Harding: "I find the said Harding is as Gilty as the Pirate Saved."

But Governor Shute was as powerless as Captain Southack to order the Cape Codders around. A proclamation the governor issued on May 4, 1717, had no more effect than the notice Southack tacked to the meetinghouse doors.

The weather on Sunday was no better, the wind from the southwest bringing more rain. Southack nevertheless gathered his men and rowed out to the wreck in the whaleboat.

As hard as they struggled to peer through the water for bags of gold and silver coins, the sea was still too turbulent for them to see anything or to attempt a dive. Frustrated again, Southack returned to Provincetown to the *Nathaniel*, moored in Cape Cod Harbor.

As the *Nathaniel* bounced in the choppy waters of the harbor, tugging at its mooring, Captain Southack sat in his cabin, carefully composing with his inconsistent penmanship and even less consistent spelling a report to Governor Shute.

Southack began by telling what he had learned of the events of the wreck, and continued with a description of his efforts.

From his two visits to the site of the wreck, Southack was beginning to comprehend the difficulty of locating the treasure from a ship whose bones were scattered far up and down the beach. He asked the governor for help: "If their be aney News by the Pirritts at boston whear the money is," he continued, "I humbley Desier Your Excellency menets [minutes] of what Place in the ship itt was in, for I am in Great hops whare the Anchors are the money is I fancy, and weather Per Mett I have Got a whale boat to fish for itt and Things for that service."

For three days and four, all week long, storm winds blew over the Cape and whipped the raw gray sea to whitecaps, still preventing Southack from beginning the salvage of the *Whydah*'s treasure. The weather was, at least, keeping the scores of villagers off the beach. As he learned more of what had happened the day after the wreck, Cyprian Southack probably began to realize that it was not the weather that was keeping the Cape Codders away, but rather the simple fact that their work was long complete.

Monday, May 6: "at Pirate Wreck this morning wind at S.E. and rain, a very great Sea on the Wreck; nothing to be done."

Tuesday, May 7: "at Pirate Wreck this morning, wind at E. Small gale & foggy, a great Sea on the Wreck. Nothing to be done there."

Wednesday, May 8: "at Pirate Wreck this morning wind att S and fogg Strong gale & great Sea, nothing to be done on the Wreck."

Unable to reach the wreck, Captain Southack sent Mr. Little and Mr. Cutler "on the cruise by land and Sea to See what they can find among Inhabitants." By Tuesday, the man who had been sent from Boston to salvage a fabulous pirate treasure "ordered Several Peices of the Wreck to be burnt for the Iron work." On Wednesday he noted in his journal that "The Gentlemen have been crusing but can find nothing, nor the people bring in nothing." Only a few timid villagers brought to Southack's lodging a cartload or two of "Small things but of little value."

Captain Southack's frustration with the weather, the wreck, and especially with the "Inhabtances" of Cape Cod was clearly evident in his next letter to Governor Shute, which he wrote on Wednesday afternoon in the parlor of Justice Doane's home.

Eastham May the 8, 1717

Maye itt Pleass Your Excellency
Sir, Captt. Gorham, Mr Litle, Mr Cuttler and Mr Russell, Gentt'men that I have Deputed, have Rid at Least Thirty miles a moung the Inhabtances, whome I have had Information of ther being at the Pirate Rack, and have Gott Concernable Riches out of her.

The Cape Codders who, Southack knew, were making fun of him behind his back now would be sorry: "I shall Mention their Names to Your Excellency in Order for a Warrant to me for bringing them for boston before Your Excellency, or as You Pleass, Sir, for all thes Pepol are very stife and will not one [own] Nothing of what they Gott, on the Rack."

Southack, who by now had pieced together most of the events of the preceding week, explained to the governor how the wreckage from the *Whydah* had been carried off, beginning with Samuel Harding.

Then he described to the governor the most outrageous affront of all to the office he represented: the coroner, who had done a "deal o' diggin" to bury the dead pirates cast up on the shore, demanded payment for his services. Southack was outraged that public money should be spent to bury criminals. He refused to pay the coroner a cent, and told the coroner exactly what he thought of him. The coroner laughed, and as payment for his work, which he "figgered" was worth £83, seized £83 worth of the 200 pounds of miserable salvage that Southack had struggled to gather along the shore during the last several days. Southack was furious.

> Sir [he wrote to Governor Shute], I am of the mind that the Curner and Jurey should have nothing for buering aney of thes men After they New them to be Pirats, and they bured but Thirteen before they new them to be Pirats. as Your Excellency Pleas, I humbley Desier Your Excellency Orders to this Afare. the Curner name is Samuell freeman for his stoping aney of the Rack Goods for Paye is very hard.

Southack finished his letter with a status report, a plea for additional assistance, and a listing of the good — and bad — Cape Codders:

> Sir, the weather has ben very bad, and Great Seas So we Can Due Nothing as Yett on the Rack with my Whale boat & men, but se the Anchor Every Loaw Watter. Sir, If some Gentt'men were Commissioned here to Give Several of Them their Oath Concerning the Rack it will be of Great Service. Sir, coll. Ottis [Col. John Otis, the Chief Magistrate of Barnstable County] and Joseph Doane Esqr. are very Good men. Sir 79 Dead man are Come a shoare out Pirate Ship to this time.

Having vented his frustration in writing to Governor Shute, Captain Southack awoke the next morning to the sound of the southwest wind's roaring through the cedars and under the eaves of Justice Doane's home. With renewed determination to wrest the pirate treasure from the wreck, and from "His Majesty's Loving subjects," he was "att

Pirate Wreck this morning att 4." But again, the wind, "at
S.W. Small gale," and the "fogg," and "the Sea being so
great could see nothing for the Sand making the water
thick and muddey," made salvage impossible.

With little else to do, Southack returned to Justice Doane's
house and wrote to Governor Shute, warning the governor
that some of the pirates of Captain Bellamy's crew had
escaped the storm in the snow and the sloop and were said
to be heading north, where they would be a danger to
shipping.

                                        Eastham May the 9 1717

Maye itt Please Your Excellency
Sir, I find by maney ways that the Pirate Sloop and Snow
Tender to the Ship Lost are bound to Cape Sables to Clean,
as for the Goods Gott out of the Rack by the Inhabantes
here, I Shall make a Dilegant Search for them. Sir If the
Pirate Sloop . . . Gos for Cape Sables our Ships from
England will be in Great Danger of faling into Their hands,
If some Care be not Taken, as Your Excellency Pleass
                                 Your Excellency Most
                                 Obed Servant
                                 Cyprian Southack

Not all the pirates, however, had sailed north. The sloop
Swan, sailing to the Cape to bring Captain Southack and his
pirate treasure back to Boston, was captured and boarded in
Barnstable Bay by none other than Captain Paul Williams,
Captain Bellamy's "Cunsatte," and robbed of all its stores
before being allowed to proceed to where the pickings from
the *Whydah* were being piled up on the shores of Barnstable
Bay.

It was now a week since Captain Southack had taken his

whaleboat across the Cape and reached the site of the wreck. Absolutely nothing had been accomplished. Cyprian Southack began to feel sorry for himself. The only cooperation the captain had received from any Cape Codder was the "plum Posset" Justice Doane's wife had given him to soothe his "Soar throte" and the "Indie-Kachoo bandanie" (West Indian bandana) that the good Justice gave to him for his sneezing and nose-blowing, for Southack, exposed day after day to the Cape's "frisking gales" and rain and "fogg," had come down with a sore throat that developed into a heavy cold in his chest.

Still Captain Southack would not give up his efforts to reap a harvest of wreckage. He continued sending the occasional cartload of sandy line and tattered sails across the Cape where they were being loaded onto the sloop *Swan*. Although he discharged "my Six whalemen" on Saturday, he noted in his journal "when we should have good Weather I know not but keep the Whaleboat in Service Still that I may see what is on the wreck Left off by the Anchor."

Monday, May 13, 1717, the wind was "NE small gale." Twelve days after he had left Boston and seventeen days after the wreck of the *Whydah*, Captain Cyprian Southack realized his mission had failed. If the great treasure still lay between the decks of the wreck, the seas off the Cape were much too rough for his divers to reach it. He had salvaged from the wreck of a treasure-laden pirate ship less than might have been recovered from a fishing boat. His luck with the pink *Mary Anne* was equally pathetic. "The wine Ship from Pirate Wreck," Cyprian Southack noted in his journal on May 5, 1717, "is South by West Dis: 10 miles where she is cast away and hath saved about 60 Pices of loine [line] with most of her Stores as I am informed." The town folk of the Southern Parish of Eastham had the Madeira safely stored away in their cellars.

He ordered the remaining cartloads of salvage from the *Whydah* to be hauled to the shore of Barnstable Bay and wrote a final report to Governor Shute:

Eastham May the 13: 1717

Hon ble

Sir, I have received your Hon^b Order of May 9: 1717 by Samuel Dogget Master of Sloop Swan and in Obedence to that Order I have Shiped all them goods that have ben Saved out of the Pirate Rack by Justice Doan and my Self on board Sloop Swan Samuel Dogget Master, on His Majestys Especial Service he being bound to Boston to follow their Your Hon ble former Orders. Tho I Putt Advertisements on each of the Motting house Dowens [doors] since After I Came to Thes Parts the Copy I have Sent you Hon. Sir I find most of the wreck is Come a shoar in Peces so am afeared that when Wether Per mott to Goe Off the Riches with the guns would be Bured in the Sand. Sir, I have Every Thing Redey to Sarch the Sand Sir, I mentioned in my Letter of May 4 to his Excellency humbley Desering him to Order a minutt from the English man Saved where the money was in the Ship when Lost that I maye be in hopes in Getting Something on a Dive off as your Hon Pleass. I can not Give aney Incuregment for Sending a Sloop on Purpose to me for the Small Matter I shall have more

Sir Y Honble Most humble servant

76 Pirates to this Day is
Bured that Come out of this
Wreck

Cyprian Southack

Captain Cyprian Southack returned to Boston, leaving Cape Codders to speculate that he had found Bellamy's gold and had secreted it away, that he had taken a Creole mistress and sailed to England to lead the life of a country squire. Old Cyprian Southack, they chuckled, was himself the King of the Wreckers.

As much as it must have delighted Cape Codders to consider this fate of the arrogant "foreigner," there was no substance behind their imaginings. In 1718, Southack was commissioned by Governor Shute to prepare a report on the need for a lighthouse at the entrance to Boston Harbor, and later that same year was sent to adjust the boundaries of Nova Scotia. Several years later, he was selected to be a member of the Council in Nova Scotia. And, of course, he continued mapping the coast of New England, including a detailed map of Cape Cod and the waters surrounding it, noting where "the Pirate Ship Whido lost." He published the highly regarded "New England Coasting Pilot" in 1720, as well as a map of "The Harbour of Casco Bay and Islands Adjacent," and "Map of Canso Harbour," and in later years "A New Chart of the British Empire in North America" and a "Map of the Sea Coast of New England." His maps and charts were relied on by navigators for the next hundred years.

At no time, from his return to Boston to his death in 1745 at the age of eighty-three, did Southack's lifestyle reflect access to a pirate hoard. In fact, not long after he returned to Boston, he ran an advertisement in the *Boston News-Letter* that "two Anchors, two Great Guns and some Jonk that came from the Wreck Whido" would be sold at "Publick Vendue" by the admiralty marshal. Several days later,

Cyprian Southack placed a personal advertisement in the
Boston News-Letter:

> To be sold by Capt. Cyprian Southack at his Hill, Sand
> for plaistering, or for Brick-work, at One Shilling a Cart
> Load, Mould Two shillings a Cart Load, and Gravel Three
> Pence a Cart Load: There being Two very good Cartways
> to fetch it, one over against the Bowling Green, the other
> by Mr. William Young the Glazier's House.

No man with a cellar full of bags of pirate gold would be
selling sand and mould — or gravel at three pence a cart
load! All that Cyprian Southack took from his hunt for the
treasure of the *Whydah* was a head cold and a desire to forget
those "stife Pepol" of Cape Cod.

CHAPTER SIX

"Ravenous Beasts of Prey"

O N SATURDAY, MAY 4, 1717, a week after the great storm, the seven pirates from the *Mary Anne*, along with the two survivors of the *Whydah*, Thomas Davis and the Indian, John Julian, "were brought upon Horseback with a Guard" from Barnstable to Boston. They were imprisoned in Boston's stone jail, placed in heavy irons in a dungeon with walls four feet thick.

Boston Town knew just how to deal with pirates.

It was to Boston that the infamous Captain William Kidd had sailed in June of 1699 when he learned that an English naval squadron was searching for him. The English Admiralty had notified all the governors of the American colonies to arrest him on sight so that "he, and his Associates, be prosecuted with the utmost Rigour of the Law." Kidd, however, was certain that he would receive protection from

the Earl of Bellomont, who was then headquartered in
Boston and was the "Captain General and Governor in
Chief of Massachusetts." Bellomont had written to Kidd "to
sail directly to Boston in New England there to deliver unto
me the whole of what Prizes, Treasures, Merchandizes, &
other things you have taken."

Fifty-four-year-old William Kidd had been a respected
and prosperous New York merchant sea captain who once
had served honorably in the king's service as a privateer
against the French. On a trading mission to London in 1695,
Kidd had been offered by the Earl of Bellomont a privateer
commission to attack pirates in the Red Sea, who had been
crippling the trade of the East India Company, and French
ships wherever encountered, since England and France were
then at war. Kidd accepted this assignment reluctantly. But
with a letter of marque and a commission from King William III, he set sail in a specially outfitted fighting ship, the
Adventure, with the blessings of the Crown, Lord Bellomont, and several other backers who were among England's
most powerful men.

At some point during his three-year voyage from London
to New York to the Indian Ocean and around the Red Sea,
Kidd crossed the fine line between privateering and privacy,
even attacking a ship under English command. Word got
back to London, and the order to capture him was spread to
every port.

Kidd was confident that he could convince Lord Bellomont he had acted within the terms of his royal commission,
and that, with his ship's hold full of treasure, his royal
backers would be pleased with the magnificent return on
their investment. Yet he was cagey enough to take some
precautions. Before sailing to Boston, he buried a treasure

chest on Gardiner's Island off the eastern tip of Long Island. For days sloops came to and from his ship, carrying away the gold bars, bags of gold dust, silver plate, sapphires, diamonds, silks, quilts, Indian brocades, calico, and spices that he was dispersing to his friends in New York for safekeeping. To Lord Bellomont's wife, Kidd sent ahead an extraordinary enameled box with four large diamonds set in gold.

Anchoring outside of Boston Harbor on July 2, 1699, Captain Kidd had delivered another gift to Lady Bellomont: gold bars sewed up in a green silk bag. This she at once sent back to him. Kidd should have realized then that something was terribly wrong. On July 6, Lord Bellomont, who had received orders from the Crown to arrest Kidd and who realized as one of the principal backers of the ill-fated expedition that his own career was in jeopardy, had Kidd captured. On July 17, the Provincial Assembly resolved that "the said Captain Kidd be put into the Stone Prison, be ironed, and company kept from him."

Bound in irons, the captain who had sailed the seas for the last three years was held for seven months in solitary confinement, treated like a wild animal.

Finally, on February 6, 1700, Kidd was locked in the steerage cabin of an English naval ship and taken to England. Incarcerated in Newgate Prison, Kidd was kept in solitary confinement for another year, until May 8, 1701, when his two-day trial began at the Admiralty Session of the Old Bailey.

Accused of killing one of his gunners in a fit of rage, Captain Kidd was charged with "being moved and seduced by the instigations of the Devil . . . [to] make an assault in and upon William Moore upon the high seas . . . with a certain wooden bucket, bound with iron hoops, of the value of eight pence, giving the said William Moore . . . one mortal bruise of which the aforesaid William Moore did languish and die," and accused also of five counts of piracy.

Kidd had long before been pronounced guilty by the English and colonial presses, which, during the years he had been imprisoned, had been filled with apocryphal tales of his savagery and cunning. As the prosecutor had stated, Captain Kidd "was an arch-pirate, equally cruel, dreaded and hated both on the land and at sea. No one in this age has done more mischief, in this worst kind of mischief, or has occasioned greater confusion and disorder, attended with all the circumstances of cruelty and falsehood."

Captain Kidd continually requested that his trial be deferred "for want of two French passes that would vindicate" him and "complained of his want of the French passes which were in the Lord Bellomont's hands." His requests were denied.

The Admiralty Court had little trouble finding Captain Kidd and several of his crew guilty and sentencing them to "be severally hanged by your necks until you be dead."

"My Lord," Kidd said after the verdict was declared, "it is a very harsh sentence. For my part I am innocentest of them all, only I have been sworn against by perjured persons." In so saying, Captain Kidd spoke the truth. The passes that would have supported his claim that he had seized ships as legal privateering prizes were found in the British Public Record Office 219 years later.

Kidd was hanged at the execution dock at Wapping on the edge of the Thames and then, as the piracy laws of the day required, his body was chained to a post until the tidal waters of the Thames ebbed and flooded over it three times. Then his body was painted with tar and bound in chains, and

Above: Captain Cyprian Southack's treasure map of Cape Cod, prepared in 1717

Left: A rendering of the *Whydah* under full sail

Above: "The Tracts of the Gallions," a 1720 map of the West Indies

Left: "Kidd at Gardiner's Island" by Howard Pyle

Opposite: An aerial view of the outer Cape, from Orleans to Provincetown

Atlantic Ocean

• *Whydah* Lost

Cape Cod Harbor

Where Captain Southack Crossed the Cape

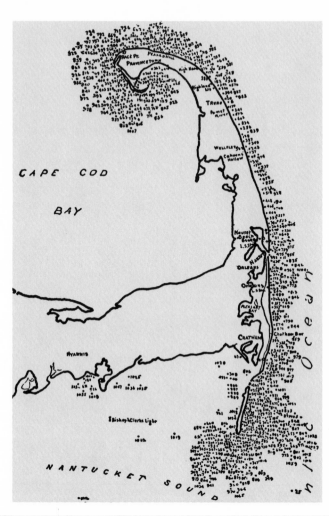

Above: The sea cliffs of Wellfleet. It was off this beach that the *Whydah* capsized.

Right and below: Pages from Captain Southack's journal

Opposite, top: Map of Cape Cod showing wrecks through 1903

Opposite, bottom: During storms, thirty-foot waves smash the Cape's outer beach where the *Whydah* foundered.

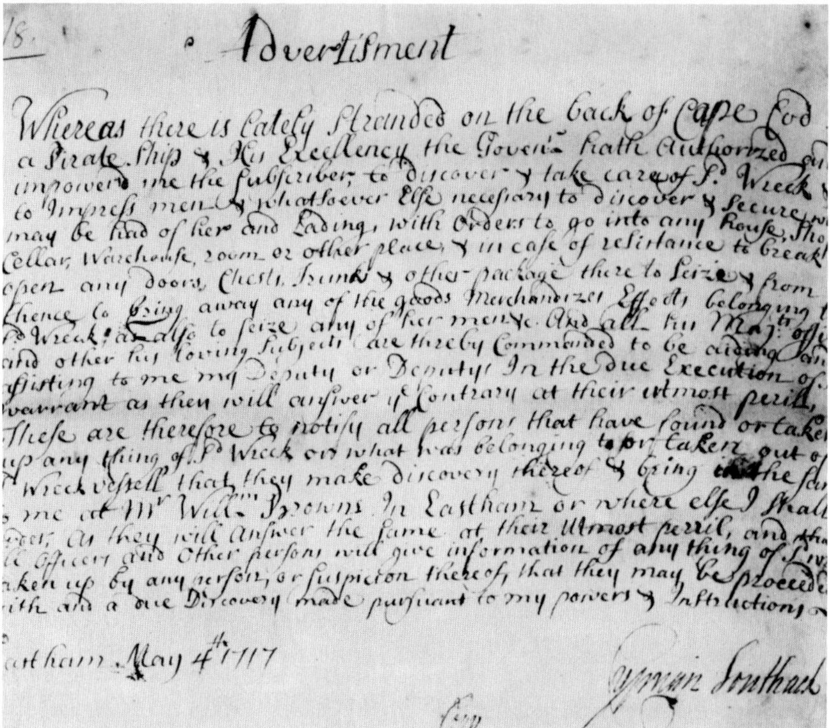
18.

Advertisment

Whereas there is lately Stranded on the back of Cape Cod
a Pirate Ship & His Excellency the Govern.r hath Authorized an
impowerd me the Subscriber, to discover & take care of S.d Wreck &
to Impress men & whatsoever Else necessary to discover & Secure
may be had of her and Lading, with Orders to go into any house, Sho
Cellar, Warehouse, room or other place, & in case of resistance to break
open any doors, Chests, trunks & other package there to Seize & from
thence to bring away any of the goods Merchandizes Effects belonging t
S.d Wreck; as also to seize any of her men &c. And all his Maj.ts offi
and other his loving Subjects are hereby Commanded to be aiding an
assisting to me my Deputy or Deputys In the due Execution of
warrant as they will answer y.e Contrary at their utmost perill,
These are therefore to notify all persons that have found or taken
up any thing of S.d Wreck or what was belonging to or taken out o
S.d Wreck vessell that they make discovery thereof & bring the sam
to me at M.r Will.m Browns In Eastham or where else I shall
be, As they will Answer the same at their Utmost perril, and tha
all Officers and Other persons will give information of any thing of s.d W
taken up by any person, or suspicion thereof, that they may be proceede
with and a due Discovery made pursuant to my powers & Instructions

Eastham May 4th 1717

Cyprian Southack

A warning to treasure hunters in Captain Southack's hand

Instructions to the LIVING,
from the Condition of the
DEAD.

A Brief Relation of REMARKA
BLES in the Shipwreck of a
bove One Hundred

Pirates,

Who were Cast away in the Ship
Whido, on the Coast of *New-
England*, *April* 26. 1717.
And in the Death of Six, who after a Fair Trial at *Boston*, were
Convicted & Condemned, *Octob.*
22. And Executed, *Novemb.* 15.
1717. With some Account of
the Discourse had with them on
the way to their Execution.

And a SERMON Preached on
their Occasion.

Boston, Printed by *John Allen*, for
Nicholas Boone, at the Sign of
the Bible in *Cornhill*. 1717

Above: Cotton Mather at age
sixty-five

Left: Reproduction of title page
of Cotton Mather's sermon
"Instructions to the Living from
the Condition of the Dead"

Below: A view of the harbor and
town of Boston in 1723

Left: Barry Clifford meeting with reporters on July 26, 1984, a week after the discovery of the *Whydah*

Below: Barry Clifford *(right)* and Captain Richard Gray of the salvage vessel with coins from the *Whydah*

hung from a gibbet on Tilbury Point, there to swing for years over the waters, "a sun drying," to be seen by every seaman sailing in and out of the Thames, to serve, as the Admiralty Court had stated, "as a greater Terrour to all Persons from Committing ye like Crimes for the time to come."

Since the capture of Captain Kidd, Boston had become known as a "hanging port." Plagued by pirates, the maritime province of Massachusetts had enacted strict laws making any act of piracy punishable by death, decreeing it unlawful for any person to "enterteyne, harbour, counsel, trade or hold any correspondence by letter or otherwise with any person or persons that shall be deemed or adjudged to be privateers, pyrates, or other offenders," and empowering the highest commissioned officer in each town and port to issue warrants for the seizure of suspected pirates. So strident was the town's hatred of piracy that it became something of a ritual for New England pirates to force their hostages to curse the Reverend Cotton Mather, the pastor of Boston's Second North Church, who frequently preached sermons about the evils of piracy. Pirates were fond of telling their captives that they would never be taken to Boston alive but "if they should ever be overpower'd, they would set Fire to the Powder with a Pistol, and go all merrily to Hell together."

By order of Governor Shute, on Monday, May 6, 1717, each of the pirates of the *Whydah* was interrogated. Each described how he had been captured by Captain Bellamy, how he "and every one of the other Prisoners were forced to Join the Pirates," and how Captain Bellamy had threatened to set them "ashore on a Moroon Island" if they "would not be easy." As they described it, the reason they "did not discover themselves to the Government when they first came ashore was because they expected to get to Boston and there Ship themselves as sailors."

Of keener interest to the governor than the pirates' stories was their account of the treasure on board the *Whydah*. Each was carefully questioned on this subject.

Young John Brown stated that "It was the common report in their Ship, that they had about 20000 Pounds in Gold and Silver."

Thomas Baker reported that "they had on Board 20000 or 30000 Pounds, and the Quarter Master declared to the Company, that if any Man wanted Money he might have it."

"The riches on board were laid together in one heap," Thomas Davis explained, although he did not know the amount of the treasure.

Peter Hoof knew more: "The Money taken in the *Whido*, which was reported to Amount to 20000 or 30000 Pounds, was counted over in the cabin, and put up in bags, Fifty Pounds to every Man's share, there being 180 Men on Board . . . Their Money was kept in Chests between Decks without any guard."

And the Frenchman John Shuan confirmed that "on board of Bellamy's [ship] there was a great quantity of Silver and Gold."

Having learned what they were after, the representatives of the governor left, and the pirates were brought back to their cell.

All summer long, the young sailors who had roamed the seas at will, who had been bound by no laws, the "free princes" of the seas as Bellamy called them — all summer long they sat alone, manacled in a damp dungeon. Their thoughts centered on escape. But bound in irons, locked in the jail, guarded day and night, they were trapped. If Captain Bellamy were alive, he would save them. But they had learned from Thomas Davis all about the shipwreck and the tragedy of that Friday night in April.

The pirates undoubtedly entertained hope that Captain Paul Williams, as soon as he learned what had happened to the *Whydah* and the *Mary Anne*, would rescue them. In fact, Williams and his crew lurked off the New England coast all summer. When they took a ship commanded by Captain Thomas Fox in July, the pirates questioned their hostages "whether any thing was done to the Pirates in Boston Gaol." Captain Fox responded that he knew nothing about them. A friend of Thomas Baker or Hendrick Quintor, "A Dutch-man belonging to the Pirates," asked Captain Fox about "his consort, a Dutch man in Boston Prison." The pirate swore "that if the Prisoners suffered they would Kill every body they took belonging to New-England."

But as the imprisoned pirates waited for a midnight tap on the bars of the dungeon, or for a smuggled message, or for Captain Williams's men to storm the old stone prison, as the weeks went by and their muscles grew soft, it became more difficult to convince themselves that their comrades would come.

In October, they learned that seven out of eight of them were to be tried for piracy.

The exception was Thomas Davis, the young shipwright. Davis had been sick when he reached Boston. His immersion in the frigid waters of the North Atlantic when he was swept off the *Whydah*, his exposure to the tempest as he and John Julian sought Samuel Harding's farmhouse, and his exertion as the two shipwrecked men helped Harding lug cartloads of treasure from the beach, had broken his health.

After his recovery, Davis was kept in the cell with the other prisoners. He was concerned from the outset that "the Pyrates in Prison suspect that he will make such discoverys as will not be pleasing to them" and was therefore "fearfull least they should hurt him, if not deprive him of life, to prevent his Testimony against them." He begged to be freed "from his Chains and Imprisonm't with the pyrates, and that he may have some Apartm't seperate from them."

Seth Smith, the prisoner-keeper at the Boston jail, recognized that Thomas Davis was a different breed from the pirates. He took Davis aside and advised him "that if he would be ingenuous & make a confession, he might save his Life, and be a good Evidence against the other Pirates in Prison." Thomas Davis told him that "he was abused by several of the Pirates that were Drowned, and was glad he had got away from them, but knew nothing against the rest of the Pirates in Prison."

A judiciary court of admiralty was assembled and held in the courthouse in Boston on Friday, October 18, 1717. The judges of the court were especially appointed to "Try, Hear and Adjudge Cases of Piracy, Robbery and Felony Committed on the High Seas" and included Samuel Shute, the governor and commander-in-chief of the province, Lieutenant Governor William Dummer, seven members of "His Majesty's Council" for the province, Vice Admiralty Judge John Menzies, the commander of His Majesty's ship-of-war, the *Squirrel*, and the collector of the plantation duties.

The court immediately issued a warrant directed to the sheriffs of the County of Suffolk requiring them "forthwith to bring into Court the Bodies of Simon Van Vorst, John Brown, Thomas South, Thomas Baker, Hendrick Quintor, Peter Cornelius Hoof, and John Shuan, from His Majesty's Gaol in Boston."

The sheriffs brought the prisoners into the courtroom, and, "having held up their hands at the Bar, the Indictment Exhibited against them by Mr. Smith, His Majesty's Advocate, was Read to them" by the notary public in a slow, flat voice that filled the courtroom:

"That such Persons, as shall be . . . found Guilty of Piracy, Robbery & Felony committed in, or upon the Sea or in any Haven, River, Creek or Place where the Admiral or Admirals have Power, Authority or Jurisdiction, by their own Confessions, or their Refusing to Plead, or upon the Oath of Witnesses by Process founded on the Authority of His Majesty's Commission or Commissions by the said Act directed and appointed, shall be Executed and put to Death."

The notary public read on and on:

"Nevertheless so it is, That the said Simon Van Vorst, John Brown, Thomas South, Thomas Baker, Hendrick Quintor, Peter Cornelius Hoof, and John Shuan, To the High displeasure of Almighty God, in open Violation of the Rights of Nations and Mankind, and in Contempt and Defyance of His Majesty's good and wholesome Laws aforesaid, Wilfully, Wickedly, and Feloniously, all and each of them, being Principal Actors and Contrivers, Associates, Confederates, and Accomplices, Did, Perpetrated and Committed on the high Sea sundry Acts of Piracy and Robbery."

The pirates understood only enough of what the notary public was reading to realize that they were in trouble.

After the indictment was read to the court, the king's

advocate, Mr. Smith, moved the court that the prisoners should plead guilty or not guilty as the Act of Parliament and civil law required.

Simon Van Vorst, on his behalf and for the rest of the prisoners, asked the court's permission to consult an attorney before pleading, so that they "might be well advised what to do." The court granted this request.

Thereafter, the prisoners were again asked how they pleaded, and each pleaded "not guilty." John Shuan, the Frenchman, made it known to the court through sign language that he did not understand what charges were being brought against him. A Boston merchant who spoke French was sworn in and read Shuan the indictment. Shuan also pleaded "not guilty."

Mr. Smith approached the bench and addressed the court.

Piracy, according to Mr. Smith, was a combination of "Treason, Oppression, Murder, Assassination, Robbery and Theft," a crime that is committed "in remote and Solitary Places, where the weak and Defenceless can expect no Assistance nor Relief; and where these ravenous Beasts of Prey may ravage undisturb'd, hardened in their Wickedness with hopes of Impunity, and of being Concealed for ever from the Eyes and Hands of avenging Justice.

"That the Prisoners are all and each of them Guilty will evidently appear to your Excellency from the Testimonies of three Persons, who belonged to the Vessel. . . . The Witnesses are here in Court, and I humbly move that they may be examined and interrogated."

Mr. Smith took his seat at the counsel table. The court asked the prisoners if they had any challenge or objection to make against the witnesses. None being offered, the witnesses were sworn in.

First appeared Thomas Fitzgerald, the mate of the pink *Mary Anne*, who testified as to the capture of the *Mary Anne* on April 26, 1717, when the pirates "all Armed with Mosquets, Pistols and Cutlasses" had "forcibly taken Command of her," with the exception of Thomas South who, soon after he came on board, told Fitzgerald of "his Intention to make his escape from the *Whido*, as soon as he could." Like South, John Shuan was unarmed, but "was very forward & active on board the Pink." Fitzgerald told how the pirates plundered the cargo of wine and took "some Cloaths which belonged to the Ship's Company," and he recounted the events of the storm and the shipwreck and the apprehension of the pirates the next day by Justice Doane. The mate's vivid account of these events included a detailed report of how Simon Van Vorst had threatened to break the cook's neck "if he would not find Liquor" and how the pirates joked that they had "got a Commission from King George" and would "stretch it to the World's end."

The next witnesses were James Donavan, mariner of the *Mary Anne* and brother-in-law of Andrew Crumpstey, the late captain of the *Mary Anne* who had died aboard the *Whydah*, and then the pink's cook, Alexander Mackconachy. Their testimony corroborated Fitzgerald's report of the capture of the *Mary Anne* and that "Thomas South's Behaviour in the Pink was civil and peaceable" and that he "behaved himself Civily." They also told how Thomas Baker threatened to shoot the cook "thro' the head, because he Steer'd to the windward of his Course."

Four more witnesses followed, all of whom had had some experience with the pirates that they were anxious to share with the court.

John Brett had been taken captive in June 1716 by Captain

Bellamy and Captain Lebous, who "Damn'd" him and "bid him bring his Liquor on board. . . . They carryed him to the Island of Pynes, and he was detained a Prisoner by them there Eighteen days." Brett recalled being threatened by John Brown, who told him "that he would hide him in the Hold, and hinder him from complaining against him, or telling his Story."

Thomas Checkley had been a sailor aboard the *Tanner*, captured in March 1717 by Captain Bellamy and Captain Lebous, who "pretended to be Robbin Hoods." He remembered that the pirates "forced no Body to go with them, and said they would take no Body against their Wills," but that John Shuan "declared himself to be now a Pirate," and "went up and unrigged the Main top-mast by order of the pyrates."

John Cole reported on the few hours the pirates spent at his house on Cape Cod after the shipwreck of the *Mary Anne*, and Justice Doane testified as to his capture of the pirates at Higgins Tavern, where "they confessed that they belonged to Capt. Bellamy commander of the Ship *Whido*, and had taken the Pink *Mary Anne* in which they run on Shoar."

That afternoon, the pirates were called before the court and asked "what they had to say for themselves."

Simon Van Vorst explained that he had been forced by Captain Bellamy to become a pirate and to join the *Whydah*'s company. He explained that he had considered telling the mate of the *Mary Anne* that he wanted to escape from the *Whydah*, but that "he understood by the Mate's discourse that he inclined to be a Pirate himself, and therefore he did not discover his mind to the Mate."

John Brown also alleged that he was forced to join the

Whydah's crew, but could produce no evidence to confirm this allegation.

Thomas South testified that he was a member of the crew of a ship out of Bristol, England, and "That he was taken by Capt. Bellamy, and forced to tarry with him, otherwise was threatened to be put upon a desolate Island, where there was nothing to support him."

Thomas Baker explained that he and Simon Van Vorst were both captured from the same ship, and that "he attempted to make his escape at Spanish Town [the old Spanish capital of Jamaica], and the Governour of that Place seemed to favour his design, till Capt. Bellamy and his Company sent the Governour word that they would burn & destroy the Town," if Baker was given refuge. Afterward, Baker continued, he would have made his escape at Crab Island, "but was hindered by four of Capt. Bellamy's Company."

Hendrick Quintor also alleged that he was captured by Captain Bellamy when his pirates seized a French vessel, that Bellamy had agreed to let him go when they reached the coast of Crocus [Caracas, Venezuela], but later changed his mind, and so "he was unavoidably forced to "Continue among the Pyrates."

Peter Cornelius Hoof's testimony followed the same lines: that he was taken by Captain Bellamy from a vessel under the command of John Cornelius, and that Bellamy's crew swore "they would kill him unless he would joyn with them in their Unlawful Designs."

John Shuan's story was told to the court by his interpreter. Shuan had been sick at the time he was captured by Captain Bellamy and he was taken "on board the Pirate Vessel at the Instance of Capt. Bellamy's Doctor, who advised him to stay with him till his Cure." Shuan explained that when he went on board the *Mary Anne* "he did not carry any Arms with him; and that he hoped by going on board the Pink he should the sooner make his escape from the Pyrates, for that he had a better way of getting his living than by Pyrating."

After the pirates had completed their testimony, His Majesty's Attorney General "in a very handsome and learned Speech" summed up the evidence and presented his concluding remarks.

Mr. Smith, His Majesty's Advocate, then stood and silently paced the floor in front of the bench before he spoke.

"May it please your Excellency:

"Their pretence of being forced out of the respective Ships and Vessels they belonged to, by Bellamy and Lebous, if it [is] true, can never excuse their Guilt, since no case of Necessity can justify a direct violation of the Divine and Moral Law, and give one the liberty of Sinning.

"That they acted freely and by their own choice is most plain and obvious, for when they had the fairest opportunity, that could have happen'd, to make their escape, if they had intended it, by means of the Weather, Wind and nearness of the Shoar, they were obstinately resolved rather to hazard the Vessel and their Lives, than lose company with the *Whido*. . . .

"As the English Trade is in the utmost danger at present in America from the prodigious Number of Ships exercised in Piracies and as Providence hath wonderfully preserved us by destroying their Capital Ship with her Numerous Crew, and hath no less wonderfully delivered into the hands of Publick Justice the Prisoners at the Bar, to teach others by their Exemplary Punishment to abhor the barbarous and inhumane practices, which have been fully proved against

them, and whereof they stand convicted, [I] humbly move
His Excellency and the Honourable the Commissioners to
proceed to pass Sentence of Death upon all and each of
them, they being all equally Guilty. To show the least Pity
in matters of this kind, where the Proofs are so full and
Pregnant, and not the least presumption in favour of the
Prisoners, would be the greatest cruelty."

The courtroom was cleared. Upon reviewing the trial and
the evidence that had been presented, the judges found
Simon Van Vorst, John Brown, Thomas Baker, Hendrick
Quintor, Peter Cornelius Hoof, and John Shuan guilty of
piracy, robbery, and felony as set forth in the indictment.
But the court concluded that Thomas South indeed had been
taken from his ship and "compelled utterly against his
Will to joyn with the Pirates. The judges therefore were
of the opinion, and accordingly voted, that "Thomas South
is Not Guilty."

The prisoners were led back to the courtroom.

"Have you anything further to say why Sentence of Death
should not be Pronounced against [you] according to the
Law?" they were asked.

The pirates could offer no other testimony than what they
had already presented at the trial.

As president of the court of admiralty, Governour Shute
pronounced its decree:

> The Court having duly considered the Indictment & the
> Proofs of the several articles contained therein, together
> with your Defences, Have found you Simon Van Vorst,
> John Brown, Thomas Baker, Hendrick Quintor, Peter
> Cornelius Hoof and John Shuan, Guilty, of the Crimes of
> Piracy, Robbery and Felony, as is set forth in the Indict-
> ment, And do therefore Adjudge and Decree, That you

Simon Van Vorst, John Brown, Thomas Baker, Hendrick Quintor, Peter Cornelius Hoof, and John Shuan, shall go hence to the Place from whence you came, and from thence you shall be carryed to the Place of Execution, and there you and each of you, shall be hanged up by the Neck until you & each of you are Dead; And the Lord have Mercy on your Souls.

Thomas South, The Court have found you not Guilty.

South kneeled, and thanked the court. "And after he was duly Admonished and had Promised Amendment of Life, he was dismissed and taken out of the Bar."

Then "Charge was given to the Sheriffs to take Special Care of the Condemned Prisoners."

The judiciary court of admiralty was adjourned for a week until Monday, October 28, 1717, at 9:00 A.M., when, pursuant to a warrant of the court, the sheriffs of Suffolk County brought the Welsh boy, Thomas Davis, from the jail to Boston's courthouse.

The court commanded silence.

His Majesty's Advocate, Mr. Smith, read to the court the indictment that had been filed against Davis, alleging that he, along with other pirates, had captured a "Free Trading Ship called the *Whido*," and that he, with other pirates, had then taken over the ship, which was used in "Perpetrating and Committing Piracies, Robberies and Depredations.

"The commission of such crimes of Piracy, Robbery and Felony committed on the High Sea," Mr. Smith concluded, looking up at the judges, ". . . admits and requires, he, the said Thomas Davis, ought to be punished by Sentence of the said Court with the pains of Death . . . to the Example and Terror of others to do, or commit the like crimes in times coming."

When the king's advocate moved the court that the prisoner plead guilty or not guilty, Thomas Davis requested that he be assigned counsel. John Valentine was admitted as his attorney. Davis then "held up his hand at the Bar, and pleaded 'Not Guilty.'"

The court was adjourned for a day until Wednesday, October 30, so that Davis and his attorney could review the indictment.

At nine o'clock that Wednesday morning, after the opening of the court, Thomas Davis was given the opportunity to make any objections to the indictment before the witnesses were examined, but neither Davis nor his attorney objected.

Mr. Smith then presented his case to the court.

"May it please Your Excellency," he began, slowly walking to the front of the courtroom. "The Prisoner at the Bar is arraigned before You, for Crimes of Piracy, Robbery and Felony by him committed on the High Sea, in Confederacy, combination and conspiracy with others like himself, i.e., Profligate and Felonious Persons; And has pleaded Not Guilty. . . .

"I humbly move, the Nature of the Crime the Prisoner is charged with, and the manner of proof adduced to convict him, may be duly considered, and if his guilt shall plainly appear by his own confession, the evidence of Witnesses, and violent necesary presumptions, that he may by Sentence of this Honourable Court suffer the Punishment which the Law inflicts."

The "Kings Evidences were called into Court."

Owen Morris, a sailor, testified that he "knew the Prisoner at the Bar" and that "he belonged to the Ship *St. Michael*."

"In the Month of Sept. 1716," the sailor explained, "[we]

left Bristol bound to Jamaica, & in Decemb. following the said Ship was taken by two Pirate Sloops, one commanded by Capt. Sam. Bellamy, & the other by Loues Lebous, about Twenty Leagues off Sabria."

The court's attention was focused on this witness as he continued his tale.

"They detained the Prisoner because he was a Carpenter & a Single Man, together with Three others of the Ships company. The Prisoner was very unwilling to go with Bellamy, and prevailed with him by reason of his Intreaties to promise that he should be discharged in the next Vessel that was taken."

Thomas Davis, who had seemed to be holding his breath, exhaled slowly and leaned back against the bench.

"The Prisoner," Owen Morris concluded, "reminded the said Bellamy of his promise; when he asked him, If he was willing to go, He answered, Yes; and then the said Capt. Bellamy replied, If the company would consent he should go. And thereupon he asked his company if they were willing to let Davis the Carpenter go? Who expressed themselves in a Violent manner, saying, No, Damn him, they would first shoot him or whip him to Death at the Mast."

John Valentine leaned over and whispered something to his client, Thomas Davis. Both seemed relieved.

Thomas South, who knew just how Davis must feel, was the next witness.

"[I] thought it not prudent to be too familiar with the Prisoner," South explained to the court, describing the period they were both held aboard the *Whydah*, "because it might tend to create a jealousy in the Pirates that [he and I] (whom they suspected because he was a forced Man) would run away together. Capt. James Williams commander of the

Ship *St. Michael* (whose Carpenter the Prisoner was) Intreated the said Capt. Bellamy when he took him to let the Prisoner go. But the Ships company would by no means consent thereto by reason he was a Carpenter; and Swore that they would Shoot him before they would let him go from them."

The court then asked Davis "to speak for himself."

Thomas Davis began talking, slowly and carefully, so that the court might understand everything that had happened to him.

He described how he and "fourteen other Prisoners were put on board the *Sultan* Galley, then under the said Bellamy's command who had taken her from Capt. John Richards: And afterwards took another Ship called the *Whido*, in which Ship to [my] great grief & sorrow, [I] was forced to come upon this Coast, where she was cast-away."

He told the court how he and "John Julian only escaped Drowning." As this account showed, he pointed out to the judges, "he was no way active among the Pirates, only as he was compelled by them."

Other witnesses confirmed that the defendant was of good character.

Defense counsel John Valentine moved "that an affidavit under the firm Seal of a Notary Publick in Great Britain, and in favour of the Prisoner should be read in open Court."

The affidavit consisted of two letters to the court on behalf of Thomas Davis.

One was from Davis's father:

To His Excellency the Governour and Council
   The humble Petition of William Davis of Bristol Carpenter and Father of the said Thomas Davis,
   Sheweth, That the said Thomas Davis from his youth up

hath been a Dutiful and Obedient son, and his life and Deportm't has been always Regular and becoming as well as Peaceable, and your poor Pet'r prays your Excellency and Honours will Compassionate him and extend your Favour and Indulgence to his son as far as shall stand with your Wisdom and Clemency.

And your Pet'r shall pray, etc.

WILLIAM DAVIS

And, a sea captain wrote to the court on Davis's behalf:

Capt. John Gilbert, Mariner, belonging to Bristol, Testifyeth and saith That he well knew Thomas Davis (son of the above named William Davis) for these seven or eight years last past, and that he has had a good Education in a Religious and Orderly Family, and his Conversation, Carriage and behavour all that while was very decent and becoming, and this Depon't has no reason to think but that he always lived a well ordered life, having never heard to the Contrary.

And further Saith not.

JNO. GILBERT

These affidavits, though, were never read to the judges, for Mr. Valentine's motion was rejected as being contrary to an act of Parliament "which directs that all Evidences respecting Pirates shall be given into Court *Viva Voce*." But the fact that there was further evidence in support of Davis must not have gone unnoticed.

Even the witnesses called to present the case against Thomas Davis confirmed that Davis had been taken prisoner by Captain Bellamy and held on the *Whydah* against his will. Yet Mr. Smith continued his case.

"[If Thomas Davis had] been really affected with so much grief and sorrow as he pretends," His Majesty's Advocate sneered, "it was not impossible for him to have made his

Escape at some of the Places where he touched before he came on this Coast, viz; Blanco, The Spanish Main, Testages and Long Island; but it is not so much as suggested, that ever he attempted it nor is it to be presumed as matters stood."

He paused dramatically.

"The spoil was not yet divided," Mr. Smith shouted, emphasizing each word, "and it is obvious he expected to receive his share.

"To conclude," he stated, walking back to counsel's table, "the Crimes charged upon the Prisoner being direct Violations of the Laws of Nature as well as His Majesty's, and the proofs adduced being sufficient to convict him, He ought to Suffer the Pains of death."

After a short debate in their chambers behind the courtroom, the judges were quite convinced that there was good proof that Thomas Davis "was forced on board the Pirate Ship *Whido* which excused his being with the Pirates," and that there was "no evidence to prove that he was an accessory, but on the contrary that he was forced to stay with them against his will." The court therefore voted that "the said Thomas Davis is Not Guilty."

When Governor Shute announced "that the Court found him Not Guilty of the crimes for which he was Indicted," twenty-two-year-old Thomas Davis fell to his knees and bowed his head.

Captured from the *St. Michael* in December 1716, held hostage aboard the *Whydah*, cursed by the band of pirates who threatened to "shoot him or whip him to Death at the Mast," cast ashore in a tempest on the Cape Cod beach, imprisoned in Boston for six months: the harrowing year-long ordeal of Thomas Davis was finally over.

CHAPTER SEVEN

"The End of Piracy"

T HE ORDEAL OF THE SIX imprisoned pirates of the *Whydah* had just begun, for frequently to study them and to save their souls came the famed Puritan ecclesiastic Cotton Mather.

Forever mindful of his imposing family heritage — his father, Increase Mather, and grandfather, Richard Mather, and maternal grandfather, John Cotton, had been towering Puritan religious leaders and statesmen of New England — Cotton Mather felt himself from birth ordained to carry on the Christian leadership of his forebears. He developed an impressive piety at a very early age, noting later in his life that he prayed as soon as he could talk. Indeed, while still a child he began his efforts to achieve a world of godliness, showing his less pious seven- and eight-year-old schoolmates their errors, rebuking them for their "Wicked Words and Ways," and writing out short prayers for them which he

"Obliged them to Pray." Young Cotton was surprised when the other students beat him with their fists, though many historians, Samuel Eliot Morison among them, have noted with glee that the "young prig" got exactly what he so richly deserved.

Cotton Mather, however, was not one to stray from his genealogical obligations of righteousness and missionary fervor. He continued his reading of fifteen chapters of the Bible every day — five in the morning, five at noon, and five at night — and preparing for his life's work in the Lord's service. Upon entering Harvard College at the age of twelve, its youngest student, he was again hazed by his classmates, whose lives he tried to better.

Mather of course became a Puritan clergyman, preaching his first sermon at the age of sixteen, presiding over the Second North Church in Boston from 1685 until 1722, and living a life of ceaseless activity in his zeal to attain the impossible goals of purity, goodness, and godliness that he set for himself and others: praying strenuously, sometimes through the night; wrestling daily with Satan, who tormented him with doubts; fasting, preaching, caring for the sick, and setting down his thoughts and principles in over four hundred published books and pamphlets. A respected religious leader of the day, Mather, nevertheless, was a difficult man for his contemporaries to understand or love; at least a hint of the reaction of one modern scholar — that Mather's life and thought "was at best the source of a profound revulsion, or at worst of an upset stomach" — seems to have been reflected in the reactions of Bostonians of the eighteenth century.

No matter what he proposed, no matter what good he attempted to do in his community, Cotton Mather encountered opposition. In a moment of frustration, he once an-

nounced to the Boston community that he was through with
offering suggestions for good works; from then on, he would
limit his proposals to people and places far from Boston.
When a parishioner questioned whether Mather was in fact
conceding defeat to Satan, the busy divine immediately
began again his vexatious efforts to relieve the poor; find
money, food, and firewood for widows and their children;
spread books, instructions, and food; maintain a small school
for Negroes, and pursue through all his days the activities he
believed were essential for a man of God to undertake.

Mather was aware constantly of his human limitations,
and agonized over the disparity between the goals he set for
himself and the life that he led. He repeatedly accused himself in his voluminous writings of being a "vile" sinner,
"feeble and worthless," beset with spiritual "diseases . . . so
complicated," he told the Lord, "that I am not able so much
as distinctly to mention them with thee; much less can I
remedy them."

If Cotton Mather saw himself as an indescribably filthy
sinner, his assessment of the rough band of pirates that had
been marched from Cape Cod to Boston on May 4, 1717,
can easily be imagined.

Just as he had made a scientific investigation of the witch
trials at Salem Village, Mather now studied and tried to
save the curious band of buccaneers cast up on the shores of
Cape Cod, or, at the very least, to prepare them "for a
Return unto God."

The good minister, who frequently preached sermons
about the evils of privateering and piracy and the wickedness of pirates, had learned that New England pirates
forced their hostages to curse him as part of their punishment. The bedraggled crew of the *Whydah* learned why

when the plump, pasty-faced, bewigged, fifty-four-year-old preacher paid his first visit.

"The Pyrates now strangely fallen into Hands of Justice here," Mather noted, "make me *the first man*, whose Visits and Councils and Prayers they beg for." Certainly after their trial, if not before, the pirates of the *Whydah* were shrewd enough to realize that it was Cotton Mather who had the power to save their lives, and so, they not only welcomed his visits, but made every effort to convince him that they had abandoned their wicked lives as a result of his good work.

During the days after their convictions, the pirates of the *Whydah* were held under guard at the North Meeting House as a warning to all who were about to sail from Boston Harbor. There, Mather labored to "Improve the Time" of the prisoners, bestowing "all possible Instructions" upon them. "All the Riches which are not Honestly gotten," Mather lectured them, as they must have thought about the scores of fifty-pound bags of gold and silver that lay in chests between the *Whydah*'s decks, "must be lost in a Shipwreck of Honest Restitution, if ever Men come unto Repentance and Salvation."

A gray, coming-of-winter Friday afternoon, November 15, 1717, was the time set for "the Execution of these Miserables."

The pirates were released from the Boston jail in the custody of dozens of "Mosketeers and sheriffs." The admiralty marshal held high his "silver Oare," an ornate symbol of the Admiralty Court's jurisdiction over crimes on the high seas, and then began leading the solemn procession through the streets of Boston, mobbed with spectators, on toward the Harbor to Scarlett's Wharfe.

Cotton Mather "took a long and sad walk with them,

from the Prison, to the Place of Executions." He spoke to each of the pirates as they were led through the streets. The minister "successively bestowed the best Instructions I could" and "prayed with them, and with the vast Assembly of Spectators, as pertinently and as profitably" as he was able. Perhaps Mather did help ease the dread of their impending fate: death at the gallows might well have begun to seem a preferable alternative to further lessons from the sanctimonious bore.

"Your determined Hour is now arriv'd," Mather declared as they left the jail, turning to thirty-year-old Thomas Baker, the tailor who had left his home in Holland a year before. "You Cry in the Destruction which GOD this Afternoon brings upon you. I am come to help you what I can, that your Cry may turn to some Good Account. How do you find your Heart now disposed?"

"Oh! I am in a dreadful Condition! Lord JESUS, Dear JESUS, Look upon me!" Baker responded in the manner he had mastered after many such meetings with Mather in prison.

"You are sensible, That you have been a very Great Sinner," Mather agreed.

"Oh! Yes; I am!" Baker consented again. "And is it possible that Such a Sinner should ever find mercy with GOD! O GOD, wilt thou pardon Such a Sinner!" he implored Mather, silently praying that the minister himself had the power to pardon him.

"My Friend," Mather assured him, "this is the very First Thing that I am to advise you of. There is a Pardon to be had!"

A flash of hope exploded in Thomas Baker's mind.

"Mark attentively, Every word that I Speak unto you."

Thomas Baker listened most attentively, straining to hear those words he wanted to hear above all others: that Reverend Mather would pardon him; that he would not be hung, that he would be set free to lead a new life. Such words were not forthcoming.

"I perceive you are in a very Great Agony," Reverend Mather stated, ending his lesson to Baker. "But, the Strait Gate must be Entered with Such an Agony."

The prisoners scuffled through the brown leaves, thick upon the cobblestones.

Seeing that he had done as much as he could for Thomas Baker, the Minister turned to "Poor Vanvoorst."

"I have been a very Great Sinner," Van Vorst confessed.

"Of all your past Sins, which are they, that now Ly most heavy upon you?" the good preacher inquired.

"My Undutifulness unto my Parents; and my Profanation of the Sabbath," the pirate responded.

This, from one of those "Barbarous Wretches," who had been engaged in the most monstrous acts of piracy, astounded the minister.

"Your Sinning against a Religious Education, is a fearful Aggravation of all your Sins. I pray you, to count it so," Mather counseled.

"I do, Syr."

"But I wish," Mather continued, "that you, and all your miserable Companions here, were more sensible of the Crime, for which you are presently to be chased from among the Living." Mather shook his head in disbelief.

"You are Murderers! Their Blood cries to Heaven against you. And so does the Blood of the poor Captives (Fourscore, I hear,) that were drown'd, when the *Whidau* was Lost in the Storm, which cast you on Shore."

"We were Forced Men," Simon Van Vorst protested once again.

"Forced!" Mather scorned. "No; There is no man who can say, He is Forced unto any Sin against the Glorious GOD. Forced! No; You had better have Suffered any thing, than to have Sinn'd as you have done. Better have died a Martyr by the cruel Hands of your Brethren than have become one of their Brethren.

"Say now; What think you of the Bad Life, wherein you have Wandered from God? Can you say nothing, that your Worthy Parents, (whom you have so kill'd!) may take a little Comfort from! have some Light in their Darkness?"

"I am heartily sorry for my very bad Life," Van Vorst confessed. "I dy with hope that GOD Almighty will be Merciful to me. And I had rather Dy this Afternoon, I would chose Death, rather than return to such a Life as I have Lived; rather than Repeat my Crimes."

Mather was not convinced the pirate had learned his lesson. " 'Tis a Good and a Great Speech; But such as I have heard uttered by some, who after a Reprieve, (which you cannot have) have returned unto their Crimes. I must, now Leave you, in the Hands of Him who Searches the Heart; and beg of Him, Oh! May there be such an Heart in you!"

As the procession passed, crowds of Bostonians stepped back and huddled together at every windy corner, as if the prisoners were dangerous beasts.

"Gold!" they shouted. "Where are the bags of gold?"

Some charitable soul handed John Brown a mug of rum which he drank in a gulp.

Others caught the eye of a pirate and called out from a

safe distance, "Throw a doubloon! A piece of eight! Here! Here!"

Cotton Mather now walked next to John Brown, the Jamaican who had joined the pirates in the winter of 1716, and who was now just twenty-six.

"Brown, in what State, in what Frame, does thy Death, now within a few Minutes of thee, find thee?"

"Very Bad! Very Bad!" Brown exclaimed.

"You see yourself then a most miserable Sinner?"

"Oh! Most Miserable!"

"You have had an Heart Wonderfully hardened."

"Ay," Brown agreed, "and it grows harder. I don't know what is the matter with me. I can't but wonder at my Self!"

"There is no Help to be had, any where, but in the admirable SAVIOUR, whom I am now to point you to."

"Oh! God be merciful to me a Sinner!" Brown tried.

"A Sinner. Alas, what cause to say so! But, I pray, What more Special Sins, Ly now as a more heavy Burden on you?" Mather questioned, still stunned by the bizarre response of Simon Van Vorst to the same question.

"Special Sins!" Brown cried. "Why, I have been guilty of all the Sins in the World! I know not where to begin. I may begin with Gaming! No, Whoring, That Led on to Gaming; and Gaming Led on to Drinking; and Drinking to Lying, and Swearing and Cursing, and all that is bad; and so to Thieving; And so to This!"

John Brown had learned quickly from overhearing Van Vorst's incorrect answer to this question. But a different response had no different effect on the Boston minister. An earthly pardon was not possible.

Mather hastened his efforts as the procession approached Boston Harbor.

"Ah! But what shall I do to be Reconciled unto GOD!" the thirty-five-year-old Swede, Peter Cornelius Hoof, pleaded with the minister, knowing that time was short.

"A Reconciliation to GOD is the Only thing that you have now to be concern'd about. If this be not accomplished, before a few minutes more are Expired, you go into the Strange Punishment reserved for the Workers of Iniquity."

Peter Hoof was shaking. Terror was in his eyes.

"You go, where He that made you, will not have Mercy on you," Mather warned. "He that formed you, will show you no favour . . . If you were to Live your Life over again, how would you Live it?"

"Not as I have done!"

"How then?"

"In Serving of GOD, and in doing of Good unto Men." Hoof had been the perfect student on the commoner's bench at the North Meeting House. Cotton Mather was delighted.

"GOD Accept you!"

"My Death this Afternoon, 'tis nothing, 'tis nothing," the pirate moaned. " 'Tis the wrath of a terrible GOD after Death abiding on me, which is all that I am afraid of."

"There is a JESUS, who delivers from the Wrath to come; With Him I Leave you."

Mather talked briefly with the twenty-five-year-old Dutch sailor, Hendrick Quintor, and finally, turned to the "last among the Sons of Death," the "poor Frenchman," John Shuan. Shuan could understand no English, so Mather spoke to him in French, assuring him that "I commit your Spirit into the Hand of JESUS CHRIST, your Redeemer."

The damp winds of November carried from the harbor the smells of tar and salt water. Gulls cried overhead. The captive sea rovers saw the masts of a fleet of merchant ships, fishing boats, and whalers moored out in Boston Harbor, the very ships that would have been prizes for the *Whydah* had the flagship not hit the shoals.

The admiralty marshal waved his silver oar. The procession stopped. The pirates, the minister, the "Moskoteers and sheriffs," and the gazing crowds had reached Scarlett's Wharfe.

The usual bustling activity at the harbor had stopped. Throngs of people gathered along the shore, and a hundred small boats filled with spectators had anchored just off the beach to get a good view.

As the pirates were rowed to Charlestown Ferry, a small strip of shoreline between the ebb and flood of the tide, they scanned the harbor to spot Captain Paul Williams and his men. Surely they would save them at the last minute. There would be a roar of the cannon of the *Mary Anne*, a blaze of gunfire, and then a horde of their comrades, cutlasses drawn and swinging, would come slashing through the crowds and free them. They would hurry back to the sloop and soon be on the high seas again.

Off a point of land below Copp's hill, "about midway between Hudson's Point and Broughton's warehouse," a gallows had been erected with a scaffold suspended from it by ropes and blocks.

Standing in the bow of a small boat in front of them as the "six pyrats" mounted the scaffold and the hangman's ropes were adjusted around their young necks, Cotton Mather, holding his Bible, his black robes blowing in the coming winds of winter, offered a prayer.

On the scaffold in their last minutes, the pirates seemed very penitent. But John Brown, maybe realizing that any more sanctimonious acting was futile, maybe having been given too much rum by the crowds as the procession made its way through the streets, appeared to Cotton Mather to have lost his mind. He broke out in furious oaths, "which had in them too much of the Language he had been used unto." Then he began reading prayers, "not very pertinently chosen," Mather carefully noted, a matter that bothered the minister no end. Finally, Brown made a short speech that greatly disturbed the hundreds of spectators gathered at the harbor and left them shivering in fear, "advising Sailors, to beware of all wicked Living, such as his own had been; especially to beware of falling into the Hands of the Pirates; But if they did, and were forced to join with them, then, to have a care whom they kept and whom they let go, and what Countries they came into."

"In such amazing Terms," Mather noted, "did he make his Exit! With such Madness, Go to the Dead!"

The other pirates said little. Simon Van Vorst sang a Dutch psalm with all his heart, accompanied by Thomas Baker. Then Van Vorst exhorted the young to lead a life of religion and keep the Sabbath and respect their parents.

And then there was silence.

The ropes holding the scaffold in midair were released.

The scaffold dropped.

As in other executions, there was "such a Screech of the women" present that it could be heard far away.

The bodies of the young pirates twitched, dancing the jig of death.

After the crowd had gone home, after the pale autumnal sun had dropped below the town of Boston, long after the end of the day, the six pirates of the *Whydah* swung above the breaking waves "within Flux and reflux of the Sea."

"Behold," Cotton Mather had said, "the End of Piracy."

CHAPTER EIGHT

"Seen in the Offen"

HERE THE STORY surrounding the sinking of the *Whydah* and the recovery of her treasure is lost in history.

"One Hundred Two Men Drowned" had been buried by the "Curner," buried back in the dunes of Cape Cod's outer beach where Maria Hallett's hut was said to be, for the *Whydah* had wrecked at her very doorstep. Goodie Hallett's meadow, Lucifer Land, this expanse of sand and dunes came to be called, an area where nothing but stubbles of poverty grass would grow; these lonely moors were said to bring bad luck to those who crossed them without reciting a prayer.

The bodies of John Brown, Simon Van Vorst, Hendrick Quintor, Thomas Baker, Peter Hoof, and John Shuan swung above the breaking waves of Boston Harbor, a warning to sailors leaving port. And there they hung until, over the years, they decayed and disappeared.

After Thomas Davis was found "not guilty" of piracy, he disappeared forever from recorded history. And John Julian, the Cape Cod Indian, had vanished from the records soon after he had been marched to Boston with the pirates and Thomas Davis. He may have escaped, or perhaps he died from his ordeal.

Cyprian Southack had reported that on "29 April Came to Anchor sum Distance from the Pirritt Rack Ship, a Very Great Sloop. After Sending his boat to the Pirritt Rack Thay Came to Saile and Chassed serveral of Our fishing Vessells, then stod in to Sea which I believe to be his Cunsatte [consort]." This was Captain Paul Williams and the crew of the *Mary Anne*, examining the wreck of the *Whydah*, and probably, with the high seas, experiencing no better luck than Cyprian Southack would have in spotting the treasure beneath the waves.

Captain Williams returned to the wreck a month later. After capturing a sloop and a schooner, he sailed into Cape Cod Harbor on May 24, 1717, about ten days after Cyprian Southack returned empty-handed to Boston. On May 25, Governor Shute sent out a man-of-war and a sloop armed with ninety men to capture him. As the governor of Rhode Island wrote upon hearing of the pursuit through the Vineyard Sound: "I hope it will please god to Bless Your Excellency's Indevours by the Sirprize and Caption of those Inhumaine Monsters of Prey so as our Navigation may be made more Safe and Secure."

Along with such other pirates as Louis Lebous and Blackbeard, who had sailed north for the summer, Captain Paul Williams haunted the waters off New England for several months. Given the readiness of bands of pirates to attempt to salvage treasure wrecks in the Caribbean, it would not have been unusual if Captain Williams, or any other pirate who learned of the wreck of the *Whydah*, attempted to salvage its cargo.

There is one last glimpse of the activities of Captain Bellamy's men who survived the storm aboard the prize ships before they are lost forever. In the two weeks after the wreck of the *Whydah*, these pirates quickly resumed their "pyrating" and captured off the coast of Maine three shallops, three schooners, and two sloops.

But, like a late afternoon fog, time obscured the fate of the great treasure of the *Whydah*.

Cyprian Southack's life is well documented. Although there is no evidence that he lived as if he had a pirate hoard stashed away, isn't it strange that a public servant whose work had always exhibited the highest degree of loyalty, of thoroughness, of perfectionism, left this assignment unfinished? Governor Shute had no interest in the broken rigging and planking, "the two Anchors, two Great Guns and some Jonk" that Captain Southack brought back with him from the Cape. He wanted the pirate treasure. Yet Cyprian Southack left Cape Cod without once having had his men dive to the wreck. "Where the Anchors are the money is I fancy," he reported to the governor time and again. Did he ever return to the outer beach of Cape Cod to explore the wreck for himself?

And what of the Cape Codders? The record is much too quiet.

A pirate ship capsized in their backyard. They learned from its two survivors that it was filled with the treasures of the Spanish Main. Several hundred Cape Codders swarmed to the scene and stripped the beach of every bit of wreckage. Knowing the nature of the vessel, they surely were not looking for halyards and dead-eyes and a quarter board.

Certainly if treasure was found, the lucky wrecker would not have revealed his good fortune to anyone, but would have secreted the plunder away. When the steamer *Onandaga* stranded on the outer beach on January 13, 1907, with a mixed cargo of wrapping paper, shoes, and screen doors, the local residents of the Cape helped themselves. It is reported that to this day some of that wrapping paper is hidden away in various Cape Cod attics. If Cape Codders stashed wrapping paper away, certainly they would have kept quiet if they had recovered bags of pirate gold. Was there a Cape Cod family that lived well for generations without any visible source of income?

Thomas Davis? John Julian? Captain Paul Williams and his crew? The pirates of the prize snow and sloop? Is it logical to assume that not one member of the pirate crews who survived the storm had an interest in what happened to the *Whydah*'s treasure? Part of the gold on board was their salary, their bonus, their commission, from nearly a year of piracy on the high seas. Now, they must have reasoned, all the bags of gold between decks belonged to them.

Two of the one hundred forty-six men aboard the *Whydah* are known to have reached shore. "One Hundred Two Men Drowned" had been buried back in the dunes. It was not unusual that not all of the bodies were recovered. In the wreck of the steamer *Portland* in 1898, in which not a single passenger or crew member survived, only sixty bodies of over one hundred fifty passengers were ever recovered. Bodies from other wrecks have been found miles down the coast from where the disaster occurred. Weeks after a wreck, a surfman patrolling a beach might come upon a hand thrust out of the sand, the rest of the corpse having been buried by the action of the sea.

But isn't it possible that at least one other of the un-accounted-for men on the *Whydah* made it to shore? Perhaps an unknown survivor, a pirate, was clever enough to realize he would hang if discovered, and therefore remained hidden. If Thomas Davis and John Julian were in satisfactory condition after reaching land, able to set out for the home of Samuel Harding two miles across the windy moors, and immediately return with him to the beach to begin removing load after wagon load of salvage, another survivor could have helped himself to the rich plunder of the *Whydah*, hiding his treasure nearby.

"Samuel Harding whoms I have Rett [written] about before," Captain Cyprian Southack reported to Governor Shute, "has a Great maney Riches he Saved out the Rack being first man their with the English man saved. His Answer is that this English man Saved Gave him Orders to Deliver nothing of the Riches they had Saved out of the wreck." And so, Harding had patiently explained to Captain Southack, there was simply no way he could let the captain have anything he had salvaged from the *Whydah* since it belonged to Thomas Davis. Did the twenty-two-year-old Welsh boy return to Cape Cod to claim the booty, or, having so narrowly escaped the gallows, would he have fled New England and the nightmare that had been his lot for the last year?

In October 1849, Henry David Thoreau left Concord, Massachusetts, to explore Cape Cod. "Wishing to get a better view than I had yet had of the ocean," he spent several weeks on the Cape, returning in June 1850 and again in July 1855.

In the chronicles of his visits, Thoreau describes the wreck of the *Whydah* and quotes a historian of Wellfleet as reporting: "For many years after this shipwreck, a man of a very singular and frightful aspect used every spring and autumn to be seen travelling on the Cape, who was supposed to have been one of Bellamy's crew. The presumption is that he went to some place where money had been secreted by the pirates, to get such a supply as his exigencies required. When he died, many pieces of gold were found in a girdle which he constantly wore."

Other historians of the Cape have recorded that a stranger returned frequently to the scene of the wreck, "operating alone at night on the beach."

Another story that has been passed down and become an indelible part of Wellfleet's local history is that of "two red-coated strangers" who tethered their horses one night long ago past the last house at Gull Pond, held a chart up to the moonlight and dug a hole, while a scared little girl, presumably the reporter of these events, "held her breath and peered at them over a window-ledge." The strangers were never seen again. Surprisingly, the story does not reveal whether or not they found Bellamy's gold, as a folktale would.

As for Maria Hallett, the record is much clearer:

It was only during evenings when fog had moved in from the sea and it was damp and dark before nightfall, or on stormy nights when the wind shook their cottages and window casings rattled, that Cape Codders would tell what they knew of Goodie Hallett.

When a dead calm held a ship in port, sailors would say that "the Old Woman has got the cat under the half-bushel," a reference to their belief that Goodie could stop the winds by putting her black cat under a "berry-bushel."

She could whistle up a tempest or hurricane. Her cat and black goat would ride on the backs of porpoises, following the ships of Wellfleet, Truro, and Eastham out to the fishing banks. When seamen would see them in the wake, they would report, "Thar be Goodie Hallett's familiars waitin' to pick up souls. Reef sail, a squall's to wind'ard!" And soon the sky would darken with storm clouds.

When a skipper caught Goodie Hallett's fancy, the "little old woman of Nauset" would whisk him from the deck of his ship at night, bridle him, and ride him up and down the Cape, returning him to his ship before morning, trembling from exhaustion.

For a century after Captain Bellamy's drowning, his lover lived inside the whale that capsized whaleboats and with a twist of its flukes stove in the hulls of ships.

In northern waters, when the whaling brigs were trapped in ice with sailors freezing in the rigging, Goodie Hallett sat in the whale with the Devil, drinking hot rum and playing cards for sailors' souls.

On wild winter nights of sleet and wind, she hung a ship's lantern on the whale's tail and piloted it close into the bars along the Cape's outer shore where the *Whydah* had sunk, luring lost ships to their destruction. Cape Codders blamed her for many of the three thousand ships driven to their doom along the Cape's outer beach.

At dusk, when storm winds lashed the Cape, riders would spur their horses past the old burial ground of Eastham and race toward the light of Higgins Tavern. The townsfolk gathered in the tavern would hear Goodie Hallett shrieking and singing out in the burying yard. "Thar be poor Goodie, dancin' with the lost souls," they would mumble as they pulled their cloaks around them and moved closer to the parlor's fire.

And even now, when a storm breaks upon the coast, there are those who know that Goodie Hallett, her black cape blowing about her, will be wandering the bluffs above the beach where the *Whydah* was lost, listening. Listening to the wind, for the sounds of dice rolling on a ship's deck, the cry from the crow's nest of "Ship, ahoy," the roar of cannon, the clash of cutlass, and the clatter of gold doubloons and silver pieces of eight, watching beyond the waves for the *Whydah* and its prizes making their way in the gale up the coast of the Cape.

CHAPTER NINE

"Important: *Whydah* Has Been Found"

Legend had it that on stormy nights the ghosts of the drowned pirates tossed old Spanish coins up through the breakers to the stranger of "very singular and frightful aspect" who walked the beach.

Reverend Levi Whitman, a minister of Wellfleet, wrote in 1793 in an account of the shipwreck that "at times to this day, there are King William and Queen Mary's coppers picked up, and pieces of silver, called cob money."

Even down to the present, after storms have stirred the surf and sand, worn, blackened coins — Spanish cobs cut from lumps of silver, the pieces of eight of pirate lore — have been found along the outer beach near where the *Whydah* was lost.

At the turn of the twentieth century, a resident of Eastham, Henry O. Daniels, walked the beach after every storm

and found hundreds of Spanish coins of various denomina-
tions. And Seth Knowles, visiting the beach over a number
of years after each nor'easter, collected a cigar-box full of
578 pieces of eight.

Every once in a while through the centuries, the *Whydah*
herself has been sighted. Reverend Whitman reported in
1793 that "the violence of the seas moves the sands upon the
outer bar so that at times the iron caboose of the ship, at low
ebbs, has been seen." Cape Codders reported to Henry David
Thoreau in the mid-nineteenth century that they had seen
the iron caboose of the *Whydah* many times at low tide. In
1923, John Nickerson spotted the remains of the *Whydah*
barely out of the water at an unusually low tide, and as
recently as the early 1950s, there were reports of sightings of
the hulk off the Wellfleet beach.

During the last decades of the nineteenth century, several
industrious Cape wreckers earned a living dragging for lost
anchors. In those days, as many as a hundred coasting
schooners might be anchored off one of the Cape's outer
towns, waiting for the wind to change. After several days,
the ships' huge anchors would become lodged in the sand.
In a high sea and strong wind, it was difficult to break the
anchors from the sand before being driven toward the bars
— so difficult that the captains would often cut their anchor
cables and sail away. At other times, the cables snapped and
the anchors were lost. Or, driven in a gale toward the Cape's
outer beach, every captain would try dropping anchor to
hold his ship out from the breakers, as had Captain Bellamy.
The bottom of the sea just beyond the bars was therefore
scattered with anchors and anchor chains, waiting for those
who knew how to raise them.

The wreckers would sail two schooners out to the anchoring grounds, dragging a quarter mile of one-and-a-half-inch whale line between them. The line hugged the bottom, held down by two sixty-pound sinkers. As the ships sailed parallel courses, the line, which was limber yet strong enough to play a hundred-barrel sperm whale, would snag any obstruction on the bottom of the sea, and the two ships would be drawn together. Then the wreckers pulled straight up on the line, and a messenger — a heavy, hinged, lead collar — was fastened around both parts of the line and slid down into the water to tighten the whale line around the object.

The real work then began. The line was made fast to the capstan through a block-and-tackle system, all hands manned the capstan bars, and slowly the object would break loose from the sand. After an hour or more of exertion, the object was at the surface and then on board. An anchor or cable could be sold to outfitters in Vineyard Haven or Boston for two to five cents a pound, a tidy profit for several hours of heavy salvaging work.

It was by just this method that, at the turn of the century, Captain Webster Nickerson of Chatham one day landed three anchors and two cannon off the outer beach. It was believed at the time that the cannon, raised off the Orleans shore, were from the pink *Mary Anne*, and that one of the anchors raised on the outer bars off Wellfleet, with a thin shank, tremendous flukes, and a ring big enough for a boy to pass through, was from the *Whydah*.

Edward Rowe Snow wrote in *True Tales of Buried Treasure* of his own efforts to salvage the *Whydah*'s treasure.

One summer in the late 1940s, he erected a fifteen-foot diving platform close to the part of the wreck that his divers told him contained the cannon. According to Snow, "The weeks went by and the expenses mounted. Diver Jack Poole tried his best to salvage a substantial amount of gold or silver from the wreck, but a handful of pieces of eight worth at most one-fortieth of the cost of the operation was all he ever brought to the surface. We almost lost one boy by drowning when he attempted to swim ashore from the platform at high tide, and then a terrific storm hit which smashed the platform to pieces."

Oscar Snow of Provincetown, a member of this expedition, saw three cannon in the area of the wreck and tried without success to pull one ashore. A few gold coins, some cannonballs, and pieces of old wood were all that was brought up.

It was Edward Snow's conclusion, after spending "the equivalent of a small treasure hoard at the scene of the pirate ship's wreck," that "it will be a very lucky treasure hunter who ever does more than pay expenses while attempting to find the elusive gold and silver still aboard the *Whydah*." Snow's reason was that "the great billows which constantly break at this part of the coast will cause all but the most determined treasure seekers to give up in despair after a few hours of being battered and tossed by the combers of Wellfleet."

And that was all.

The *Whydah* had drifted into the folklore of Cape Cod, one of the ghost ships of the outer bars, when on November 7, 1982, Barry Clifford, a thirty-seven-year-old Martha's Vineyard diver and salvager, announced that he would find the ancient wreck.

For five years, he had researched the history of the *Whydah* and lined up investors for a treasure expedition. He had spent most of the summer and fall of 1982 working with sophisticated metal-detecting equipment, making hundreds of passes over the outer bars off Wellfleet's Marconi Beach, and, using Captain Cyprian Southack's chart as a starting point, conducting surveys from the beach. From his research and field work, he was convinced that seven hundred yards off the Cape Cod National Seashore, in twenty feet of water, under five to ten feet of sand, lay the remains of the *Whydah*.

Out of several test holes at the site he recovered a clay pipe stem, two shards of gray glazed pottery, and some brass, chisel-type nails, which, when tested, dated to the early eighteenth century. Printouts from his electronic surveys revealed large pieces of iron hidden under the sand, iron objects that probably weighed from 1000 to 2000 pounds apiece, which, he concluded, must be cannon and anchors from the pirate ship. Moreover, his electronic equipment indicated that the underpinnings of the ship were held together by thick cords of rope, not the metal cables used in a later day.

"We are absolutely sure this is the *Whydah*," the diver told reporters. "There's no question. This is the most famous pirate ship in the world and we've hit it. When we tried to figure out how much it could be worth, the amount went right off the calculator." The newspapers reported him as speculating that, if intact, the treasure would be worth at least $80 million and perhaps as much as $400 million.

"It's been on my mind since I was a kid," Barry Clifford explained with contagious enthusiasm. "I first heard about the *Whydah* when I was a kid. My uncle, Bill Carr, who was a kind of a soldier of fortune himself, told me the tales of the *Whydah*, the pirates, and the treasure on board. I think I knew even then that some day I'd have to try and find it."

While a lifeguard on Cape Cod in the 1960s, Clifford had

taken up scuba diving. Every once in a while, he recalled
with amusement, he would kill a small shark while diving
and attach it to a buoy. Later, after the beach had filled up,
"I would swim out with a knife between my teeth and
thrash around with the shark." His audience watched in
awe.

A football star, marathon runner, rodeo rider, power-lifting
champion, and speed skier while attending Western State
College of Colorado, Clifford graduated, as he said, "a terrific skier with a degree in sociology. I had no idea what I
was going to do with my life. All I knew was I was having
a lot of fun and I didn't want it to stop."

He married a champion skier, they had two children, and
he worked as a Boy Scout administrator and then as a high
school physical education teacher. After his marriage ended,
he began buying land and building houses on Martha's
Vineyard. "Between 1971 and 1978 I built a million dollars'
worth of property. Making money was never that difficult
for me."

In his spare time, he dove the waters of the Cape and
Vineyard looking for lost ships. He had discovered the *Agnes
Manning*, a four-masted schooner that sank in the late 1800s
off Pasque in the Elizabeth Islands, and the wreck of the
105-foot *General Arnold*, which sank off the coast of Plymouth in 1778.

When the classes of schoolchildren he spoke to asked if
he had ever been scared while diving, Clifford replied that
yes, on one occasion he had been very frightened, but that
he would rather not talk about it. Invariably, the children
begged him for the details, and he would tell them about
the day he was diving on the *Agnes Manning*, the day something snared him on the wreck. Turning, he saw through

the cold green waters that his diving belt was hooked by the long finger of a human skeleton. On that bony finger, he told the wide-eyed students, was a gold ring. To free himself, he had to snap the finger off. Later, he said, he found that " the ring fit perfectly," and he would then hold up his hand to show the children the gold ring he wore.

It was after researching the wreck of the *Whydah* for several years that he tracked down Captain Cyprian Southack's letters and journal, which, he said, was like finding a compass. "He told us where the ship was and why he couldn't get to it. I said, 'Oh my God, I can't believe it. The treasure is still there!' " It was Clifford's belief that the Cape Codders had merely salvaged the flotsam and jetsam that washed ashore when the *Whydah* broke up, that the treasure immediately had sunk to the bottom of the sea and there remained.

Clifford made "an absolute commitment" to search for the wreck of the old pirate ship, arranging his real estate and building business so that he could devote the next five years to his quest, searching for the lost pirate gold.

On November 22, 1982, Clifford filed suit in the United States District Court in Boston, laying claim to the wreck and any treasure he might find on it. Two days later a deputy United States marshal, television cameramen, park rangers of the Cape Cod National Seashore, and reporters watched as three of Clifford's divers swam a half mile out to sea off the National Seashore beach in Wellfleet, where they anchored a large orange buoy. Attached to the buoy in a waterproof container was an order of the court, naming Clifford guardian of the wreck until title to it could be awarded in accordance with federal laws. Also attached to the buoy was a poster to ward off the claimants that Clifford's attorney predicted would soon "be crawling out of the wood-work," warning that tampering with the wreck was a crime punishable by imprisonment and fines. "We're watching," Clifford said.

When the divers swam back to shore and climbed out from the breakers, they handed Barry Clifford a bag of coin-shaped chocolates wrapped in gold foil. "Come back next year," Clifford said with a laugh, as he shared the chocolates with the reporters, television crewmen, and Seashore rangers. "Maybe they'll be real."

Clifford told the reporters that he would spend the winter preparing for the salvaging operation. He had an operating budget of half a million dollars a year, and predicted that the entire salvage operation would "take a minimum of three years, and probably five." A grid map of the site had been prepared, and everything taken from the sea would be labeled with a number noting exactly where it was found. "We know what we're doing," Clifford said. "This is no Boy Scout trip. We really did this right." His attorney added that the purpose of the exploration was not merely to find pirate gold. "We want to make that clear. It's not like we're going down there to rip the ship apart and take off with the gold. This is an archaeological project." Clifford had already talked with officials of the Cape Cod National Seashore about displaying artifacts from the wreck and founding a maritime museum focused on the discovery of the *Whydah*.

Just as in the days of Governor Shute and Cyprian Sou-thack two and a half centuries earlier, the Commonwealth of Massachusetts, learning that a pirate treasure off its shores might have been located, lost no time in asserting its claim to the ancient hoard. The attorney general rushed to file suit in the Barnstable Superior Court to have the shipwreck declared an underwater archaeological resource, and an action was begun in the United States District Court to give Massachusetts rights to one quarter of whatever Clifford salvaged.

Clifford's attorney was just as quick to dispute the claim, saying that the questions surrounding the salvage may go "all the way to the U.S. Supreme Court. The state does have title to the sea bed. That's no problem. But we don't think that means the state has title to whatever drops on the sea bed. The three-mile limit is clearly in effect, there's a whole body of case law pertaining to salvage, and it's purely within the federal domain."

Under a law enacted in Massachusetts in 1973, the Board of Underwater Archeological Resources had been created to oversee the excavation of any historically significant shipwrecks in coastal waters of the state. According to one of the sponsors of the law, "we did have [the *Whydah*] in mind. I felt that once it was found, we ought to have some kind of law." In 1983, for the first time since enactment of the law, the board was funded so that it could oversee Clifford's salvage operations and protect the state's share of the treasure, which the press was estimating might be worth as much as $50 million.

On February 25, 1983, the board met to review Clifford's plans for salvaging the *Whydah*. Several days later, his company, Maritime Underwater Surveys, Inc., was granted a special permit to explore a two-square-mile area of the ocean off Wellfleet, and to salvage whatever was found. The permit was conditioned on compliance with a number of requirements, which included allowing a member of the board to observe the salvage at any time, meeting with the board regularly so that it could monitor and evaluate the operation, hiring a marine archaeologist approved by the board, and submitting a yearly budget so that the board could confirm that there were enough funds available to properly undertake the project. Although still in court disputing the Commonwealth's claim to any of the treasure, Clifford readily agreed to these conditions.

Exploration of the site began on May 13, 1983.

The area Barry Clifford had selected to search for the *Whydah* was the two square miles of ocean surrounding the spot Captain Cyprian Southack had marked on his map: "The Pirate Ship Whido lost."

"Every time I look at the map." Clifford remarked, bending over a copy of Southack's chart, "I see something different. That old Cyprian Southack knew what he was doing. It's a very accurate map. Amazingly so."

"He was a precise man," Clifford said of Southack after reading his letters and journals and talking to some of his descendants. "If anyone back in 1717 could be believed, it was Cyprian Southack." Clifford took the various points described by Southack and "it all just triangulated. Boom."

It was exactly two miles from this site to the location noted on an 1858 map of the outer Cape as the homestead of "S. Harding," probably a descendant of Samuel Harding, the first man to reach the wreck of the *Whydah*. With the help of surveyors, Clifford located the site of Harding's house, even finding old pipe stems and pottery on the property. "At 5 morning, Came the English man that was Saved out of the Pirate Ship, Came to the house of Samuell harding, Two miles from the Rack," Southack had recorded in his journal. It was "3 miles ½ by land from the Wreck to Billingsgate," the old sea captain noted in describing the cartloads of wreckage hauled across the Cape; the site selected by Clifford was exactly three and a half miles cross-country from Billingsgate, now Wellfleet Harbor. And it was twenty-five miles by sea from the site to Provincetown Harbor, where the sloop *Nathaniel* had moored while Captain Southack explored the wreck. "[It] is very dangerous to have a vessel on the sea board side to take them things in," Southack had written, "no Harbour in 25 miles of the wreck."

Treasure hunting had changed from the days when William Phips scanned the Bahama Banks off Hispaniola for "a Rock wch . . . apeeres Like a boate Keele up," which was said to mark the spot where the Spanish galleons went down, and from the days when Captain Cyprian Southack peered over the side of his whaleboat through the heaving sea, looking for bags of gold.

Barry Clifford's expedition was based on state-of-the-art electronic technology that had been developed for military navigation and oil exploration.

Over the bottom of the sea, in a grid pattern defined by buoys, for weeks on end one of Clifford's supply boats towed back and forth a magnetometer that could sense vibrations in the magnetic fields around iron objects. Readings were transmitted through a cable to the towing vessel, where an operator noted each anomaly, or "hit," as the crew called them. The hits were registered on a print-out and plotted on a grid map.

Bottom-penetrating sonar, using sound waves and echoes, was also used to locate buried objects. A "boomer" was towed behind the search vessel, sending out sound pulses that an instrument on the vessel's hull was tuned to receive. The pulses penetrated the sand and were reflected back by whatever hard objects they struck. A computer measured the minute variations in the time it took for the sound waves to return from the object they struck, and created an echo picture of the object that revealed its approximate shape, size, and depth under the sand.

After an area of the sea had been carefully surveyed and the hits recorded, an aquaprobe — a very long, thin tube — was inserted into the sand in spots where anomalies had been pinpointed to determine the depth of the objects. Exploratory holes could then be blasted in the sandy floor of the sea by propwash deflectors. These devices, nicknamed mailboxes, were two large elbow-shaped metal tubes that fit snugly over the twin propellers of the search vessel. The ship was securely anchored over the place where the hole was to be dug, and the engines started with the propellers in gear. The powerful streams of water from the propellers were directed straight down through the curved metal tubes, with the giant water jets blowing a crater in the sea bottom. Within a half hour, the mailboxes could excavate a hole about twelve feet deep and thirty feet wide. A conveyor lifted material from inside the hole to the boat, where artifacts could be separated from the sand and mud.

After the holes were dug by the propwash, divers could do more delicate digging, using their hands or Ping-Pong paddles to fan away the sand. Underwater metal detectors located smaller objects, and various blowers and airlifts dislodged the sand from the artifacts. Electronic ranging devices employing radio signals from fixed points could help the divers return day after day to within three feet of a particular spot where they were working.

But even this type of equipment did not make treasure hunting simple. The magnetometers could not obtain accurate readings through too much sand, the penetrating sonar equipment would have to be right above an object to detect it, and the mailboxes, unless used with the greatest care, could "be as destructive," Clifford commented, "as driving a bulldozer through the Museum of Fine Arts. . . . We've got to be very careful and proceed very slowly or we could make a hell of a mess.

"People get the idea that you just put on tanks, dive down, and there's a mermaid sitting on a treasure chest," Clifford said as he laughed, pushing back his baseball cap, "but it's not that easy."

In fact, this particular stretch of coast, with its treacherous currents and tides, and storms that lash the dunes and bluffs, made the search an especially difficult undertaking.

A few miles south, down the coast, a pair of brick lighthouses had been erected in Chatham on the bluffs overlooking the sea. In 1870, the lighthouse keeper noted in his log that the towers were exactly 228 feet from the edge of the fifty-foot bank that dropped to the ocean. In December 1874, he measured again; the distance from the towers to the bank was now 190 feet. From then on, he kept measurements after each storm. Three years later, the distance was 95 feet. Six months later it was 84 feet. Alarmed by this rate of erosion, the federal government ordered construction to begin across the road on two new lighthouses. The work began none too soon. Four months later, the distance to the bank was down to 59 feet, and on December 31, 1877, 48 feet 9 inches. On December 15, 1879, the old south tower went over the bank, followed within a year by the north tower. In less than a decade, the sea had chewed 228 feet into the land, straight through a fifty-foot bluff.

Not far to the north of where the *Whydah* was lost, at the Cape Cod Light on the sand cliffs of Truro, erosion can be as much as eight feet a year. Since the tract of land on which the lighthouse sits was purchased in 1787, over seven acres have been consumed by the sea.

On the tableland above the very beach where the *Whydah* foundered, Guglielmo Marconi in 1902 erected four transmitter towers for his first successful transatlantic wireless station. From the towers, a hallway led eighty feet seaward, ending one hundred feet from the edge of the sea cliffs. Today, the remains of the hallway stop after twenty feet, right at the brim of the cliffs. The sea since 1902 has claimed 160 feet of the tablelands, which at that point are well over a hundred feet high.

With an average annual coastal erosion rate of three and a half feet along these outer shores, the beach where the Cape Codders had scurried about to salvage wreckage from the *Whydah* in 1717 was probably over nine hundred feet out to sea in 1983.

What the sea stole from one part of the coast it gave to another. The ceaseless offshore currents carried tons of sand and silt to the great Provincetown hook and to the long sandy finger of Monomoy Island, which grew as rapidly as other sections of the beach were destroyed. So strong were these offshore currents and so great the quantity of sand they carried that the divers found that the holes they blew in the sand with the wash from the ship's propellers, holes that were ten feet deep and thirty to fifty feet wide, were covered over within a day, so that they were indistinguishable from the rest of the floor of the sea.

This was the coast where the divers would be working, here twenty feet beneath the surface of the ocean where there was nothing but water and sand. Every part of the centuries-old wreck either had been carried away by the currents or had drifted down through the decades, down through ten to twenty feet of sand before reaching a floor of clay and cobblestones.

Every morning, Barry Clifford and his men loaded their gear aboard a twenty-five-foot Boston Whaler named the *Andrew Crumpstey* after the master of the pink *Mary Anne*, captured by Captain Bellamy several hours before the *Whydah* sank. By the time it was filled with scuba tanks, wet suits, the magnetometer, bags of supplies, and six or more divers, the *Crumpstey* was riding alarmingly low in the water. Clifford gunned the twin 150-horsepower outboards so that the boat hydroplaned over the shallows of Nauset Harbor. "We had less than ten inches of water there, folks," he would announce with a smile, as the *Crumpstey* bounced and slapped out the inlet to the ocean, and, at forty knots, raced the three miles up the outer beach, just where Cyprian Southack had rowed in his whaleboat nearly three centuries before.

Anchored half a mile off the beach was the mother boat, the sixty-foot *Vast Explorer II*. Built for the navy as an ocean research vessel in the 1970s, it had been fitted with two huge pipe elbows that slipped over its propellers to direct the wash from the dual 250-horsepower diesel engines straight down into the water.

Most of the crew members were friends from Barry Clifford's college days, reunited after almost twenty years for the ultimate adventure. There was John Levin, a retired judge from Colorado who used to arm himself and go out with the police on drug raids; Robert McLung, Clifford's college roommate, who had been the sheriff of Aspen; Bill Dibble, a Marine jet pilot who had flown more than one hundred missions over Vietnam; Todd Murphy, a member of the Green Berets' combat scuba team; and Trip Wheeler, a rodeo rider and motorcycle racer.

Twenty-two-year-old John F. Kennedy, Jr., the son of the late President, was the first mate of the *Vast Explorer* that summer. A graduate of Brown University, Kennedy had met Clifford on Martha's Vineyard several years before and found his confidence infectious. "That optimism spreads to everyone," Kennedy explained. "We started talking about diving, and through a shared interest in it we became friends. He was telling me about the *Whydah*, and he said, 'If you want to do some diving, that's fine.' How often do you get to do something like dive a shipwreck?"

Veteran treasure salvor Mel Fisher was a consultant to the expedition. It was Fisher who helped salvage the great Spanish plate fleet that Samuel Bellamy had sought before he turned to piracy. And it was Fisher who would salvage the *Nuestra Señora de Atocha*, the richly laden Spanish galleon whose sinking in 1622 devastated the Spanish Court and caused a depression in Europe. Fisher's top man was hired as Clifford's project director.

After three weeks of electronic survey work and charting, Barry Clifford reported that he and his crew had found "small hits all over the place" in a scatter pattern of wreckage. "I'm positive we will hit the wreck. We have found about 150 anomalies under the sand. We're pinpointing those now," using a computer to assist in plotting each of these hits on maps and charts.

It was like working with a modern-day treasure map. "We have to excavate every X before we know what is where. We are pretty sure we know where the main concentration is. We have got the wreck; we're positive we've got the wreck."

The crew's hope was to discover something that would prove conclusively that it was the *Whydah* they had found. "Our goal this summer is to ID the ship. If we find the pot of gold at the end of the rainbow in the process, well, that's OK too.

"We are getting really itchy. I guarantee you that I'm going to find the *Whydah*. This is not any kind of a show or a Barnum and Bailey act. I have completed every salvage project that I have started."

Yet by early summer, some were saying the *Whydah* expedition had indeed turned into a show. Clifford had tried to downplay his project for several months. But by June, he was "chomping at the bit." "It is just too much fun not to let everyone in on it," he said as he invited the press and television crews to watch his divers at work.

A flotilla of small boats and planes filled with sightseers surrounded the *Vast Explorer* each day, with groupies on the shore spying on the divers through binoculars. "For a while," Clifford said, "I couldn't go anywhere without people mobbing me. It got to be a little annoying. But then I realized people were looking at me as some kind of hero. I was doing something they couldn't do. They were rooting for me."

The staff archaeologist, Edwin Dethlefsen, remembered that when he arrived in the summer of 1983 "there was a great deal of excitement. They threw a big lawn party. There were lots of pretty girls around. Barry was handing out T-shirts and caps with the company logo on them. It was a very festive atmosphere. I thought, 'Gee, this might be interesting.'"

Soon, however, archaeologist Dethlefsen began to worry about the operation. "The whole thing was thoroughly disorganized." In Dethlefsen's opinion, the public relations aspects of the expedition had taken precedence over the search for the *Whydah*. "The press thing is focal," he recalled, "central to the whole issue. The courting of the press, all the good-looking ladies, all the camp followers on board. The publicity got out of hand." Dethlefsen soon resigned from the project.

As the summer wore on, as the press grew skeptical about the *Whydah* expedition, as more attention was focused on its lack of discoveries, Clifford seemed to become even more confident. "I think we're the ones to do it," he said. "We've got all the right equipment, all the right people. We've been paying our dues handsomely for the past few years and now it's time to collect. We're going to find the *Whydah*. If it's out there, we're going to find it, unless Bellamy's ghost drops the anchor on me. We believe in what we're doing. This is not just hype. This is the real thing. I've sacrificed virtually everything to get involved in this project and if I didn't believe I would be successful I wouldn't be out there. You have to make a 100 percent commitment and that's what I've done."

By the end of July, in the midst of all the publicity the expedition was receiving, the first of several other treasure hunters emerged. The Board of Underwater Archeological Resources received a petition for the salvaging of the *Whydah* filed in the name of Old Blue Fishing Company.

The principals of Old Blue included William Crockett of Chatham, Massachusetts, who worked as a contractor in home renovation and said he had been doing field work and research on the *Whydah* since 1971; Donald Chalker, also of Chatham, who had been a diver with the offshore oil industry; Kirk Purvis, experienced in vessel recovery; and

Dr. David Switzer, a marine archaeologist at Plymouth State College.

The men had conducted preliminary surveys of the waters from the Marconi beach in Wellfleet to Nauset Light in Eastham. Within a one-mile radius of Clifford's site, they had discovered eight wooden wrecks, none of which they believed to be the *Whydah*. The site Old Blue Fishing Company selected was a half mile to the south of where Clifford was working, 800 to 2000 feet off the beach. The wreck of the *Whydah* was believed to be scattered in a northeast pattern over this site. "It is a classic type of wreck where she hit the barrier beach, breaks up, and comes right in," Crockett told the board.

Crockett relied on many of the same documents that Clifford had examined but interpreted them differently. The *Boston News-Letter* of April 29–May 6, 1717, had reported that the *Whydah* was "cast onshore in a storm on the back side of Cape Codd, against the Middle of the Table Land." The tableland, Crocket believed, was a two-and-a-half-mile stretch of ocean bluffs near the present Eastham-Wellfleet border. Crockett had "ranged the beach" in this area and found two nails and three pottery fragments that he presented to the board, and that the board, upon examination, determined were over one hundred years old.

Yet another group, the Ocean Marine Diving Company, headed by William Daniels of Chatham, and Matt Costa and Oscar Snow of Provincetown, told the board that it intended to apply for a site, "but you can rest assured," the men said, "it is a long way from [the] sites" of Barry Clifford and Old Blue Fishing Company. Daniels added that in 1969 he dove in the area Clifford was exploring, and he did not believe the *Whydah* was there, suggesting also that Old

Blue Fishing Company may have located the pink *Mary Anne*.

At the same meeting of the board, Barry Clifford requested an extension of his search area. "We have discovered parts of the wreck to the south and possibly to the north," he told the members of the board. "We'd like to at least be allowed to explore the possibility of these being related to the ship and our site. It would be tragic to divide what may be the only pirate ship in the world that has been found."

Clifford asked permission to work in the three-mile area south of his original claim, the same location Old Blue Fishing Company was after. "I am sure there are parts of the wreck in the area," Clifford continued. "We've done specific mag work in this drift pattern. I think the historical evidence is the strongest evidence here," he said, referring to Captain Southack's report that the wreckage was scattered for four miles down the beach. "It is very important that we secure this area."

The board told Clifford that his original permit had been for a specific wreck, and that if he could document that "it broke up, it falls under your permit." It tabled the other two applications until a public hearing could be held in Boston later in the summer.

With renewed determination born of the new competition and the doubts being cast on their work, Barry Clifford and his divers decided to explore some of the largest anomalies that had shown up on the computer print-outs to try to find a cannon or anchor to identify the wreck. "If we are able to determine the identity of the ship on the first dig," Clifford said, "we will cover it up and request a meeting with the Board. We're simply trying to ID the wreck site. I think it is going to take several years to completely survey the area.

What we have got here is a sand wreck. There is nothing visible at all. In order to come up with artifacts, we are going to have to dig."

At the bottom of the first test pit, beneath ten to twelve feet of sand, the divers on August 4, 1983, retrieved a ship's rudder strap, a twenty-eight-foot mizzen stay used to support the front mast of a ship, bronze chisel-point nails, and fire brick. The finds were certainly not bags of coins or bar silver, but Clifford was as ecstatic as if they were. "It is perfect," he exclaimed. "It is like a time capsule. Historically, it is exactly where it should be." The artifacts would have to be tested to determine their age, but they appeared to be the kind of materials that indeed could have come from the wreck of the *Whydah*. According to Clifford, a member of the Board of Underwater Archeological Resources aboard the *Vast Explorer* when these discoveries were made "just freaked out when he saw the stuff."

This was to be the high point of the first diving season.

The board soon assigned the area to the north of Clifford's site to Ocean Marine Diving Company. A one-mile claim to the south of Clifford's was granted to Old Blue Fishing Company. A buffer zone of four tenths of a mile was established between each claim where no one was allowed to dig.

Clifford filed suit against the other two diving companies, calling them "claim-jumpers" and "thieves," and warned of a "gold rush" by more treasure hunters that could damage the coastline. The Ocean Marine Diving Company filed with the Wellfleet police a complaint against Clifford when early one morning the *Vast Explorer* was observed anchored right in the middle of its claim. "It is a big deal," William Daniels objected. "They can work all night there." Clifford responded that the *Vast Explorer* often moored there because the divers that lived on board frequented the Wellfleet Beachcomber, a disco several hundred yards down the beach. Clifford in turn accused Daniels of purchasing the artifacts he had shown to the board. Daniels scoffed at the air of mystery Clifford had created around his discovery of the treasure chart of Cyprian Southack, which Daniels said could be found on the placemats of half the restaurants on the Cape.

In November, the United States District Court in Boston upheld the validity of the 1973 Underwater Archeological Resources Act, approving the claim of Massachusetts to one fourth of whatever treasure was salvaged from the *Whydah*. "This legal stuff drives me crazy," Clifford complained. "It's so unjust. It has made me a wild man at times."

But even more depressing for Barry Clifford was the end of the summer and the end of the diving season, when the crowds had left the Cape and the coming of winter was in the roar of the breakers. "This is not a good time for me. I get so restless when the winter closes in, and everybody goes away."

When the diving season began again late the next spring, Clifford for several months seemed to shun publicity as much as he had courted it the previous year.

As it happened, it was the first day that summer that television crews were aboard the *Vast Explorer,* Thursday, July 19, 1984, that would be the turning point in his expedition. He had promised to take NBC reporter Nancy Fernandes and her television crew out on a dig to do a feature on the *Whydah*. When Thursday arrived, Clifford tried his best to delay. "We'd been digging up bombs, were flat broke, and had one more site to dig that had high potential." He was

afraid that once again — but now in front of national television cameras — his crew would come up only with bomb
shells, relics from years of artillery practice at an old army
camp in Wellfleet. To distract the television men, he took
them out to sea in the *Crumpstey* to watch some whales,
reluctantly returning to the *Vast Explorer* as the morning
wore on.

The mailboxes of the *Vast Explorer* blasted out a test pit.
Once the sand had cleared, the divers put on their scuba gear
and went overside, their air bubbles popping to the surface.

They entered the test pit. "It was just filled with treasure!"
Clifford recalled. "It was that simple."

NBC reporter Nancy Fernandes was watching on the
TV monitor aboard the *Vast Explorer.* "There was a big
piece of something. The diver said it was a cannon. When
more sand was blasted away the other artifacts became
visible."

On the deck of the *Vast Explorer*, Clifford chipped at one
of the encrusted masses recovered from the test pit. "At first
I'd thought it was an odd-shaped shell. But as I succeeded in
loosening it, I could see it wasn't. I held the coin in my
hand and flipped it over. There was a silver cross on it and
clearly visible, a date: 1684."

A summer storm had stalled over the Cape all morning,
with thunderheads lifting over the horizon. "The sky had
been pitch black. And when I found the coin, there were
terrific claps of thunder — the spirit of Sam Bellamy, perhaps? I'll never forget it: black sky, black ocean, and white
cracks of lightning in the sky; the white cliffs of Wellfleet
on the shore nearby."

As the crew passed the silver 2-real piece from hand to

hand, "the whole project changed at that point. We all went crazy. I felt like I was breathing pure oxygen. It was like being on the highest mountain, breathing the purest air."

In the twenty-foot test pit, fifteen hundred feet off the beach, the diving crew discovered cannons, heavily encrusted cannonballs, old swivel guns, a flintlock pistol, a rusty cutlass, silver "pieces of four," a trigger guard from a musket, and even a shoe "with toe prints still in the leather," a relic of one of the pirates who had run over the decks of the *Whydah* 267 years before.

Led right to the center of the site where the *Whydah* overturned by the trail of wreckage discovered during the 1983 diving season, Clifford and his crew were shocked, stunned by what they had found. "At that point we just closed the pit back up. We left the pit filled with treasure. We found much more than we ever expected. You could see all the stuff sticking out of the sides of the pit. The ship had never been touched. It scared the hell out of us.

"We dug in the area we thought would do the least amount of harm and in this area the pit is completely filled with artifacts. This is way beyond me. I never expected to find this concentration."

On Monday, July 23, 1984, the Board of Underwater Archeological Resources received a telegram from one of its members who had been vacationing on Cape Cod: "IMPORTANT: WHIDAH HAS BEEN FOUND."

News of the find was broadcast nationwide by NBC, and the AP wires carried the story: "Wreck Found off Cape Cod May Contain Pirate Treasure."

Clifford was convinced that the ship of his dreams had at last been discovered. "When we found the first coin this summer there was no question about it." Three of the coins were dated 1715, and one was a 1684 French coin with a hole through it. "So we've got four coins suggesting that we have a wreck that has circulated money before, unlike a Spanish galleon that would have had all one mint basically coming out of one area. This suggests very strongly to us that we have the right wreck. Not only that, this is exactly the point where Cyprian Southack said the wreck was. Eventually there will be enough circumstantial evidence and there won't be any reasonable doubt at all."

Barry Clifford was in his element. A week after the discovery, on July 26, 1984, in the East Indian Room of the Peabody Museum in Salem, where a special meeting of the Board of Underwater Archeological Resources had been called, dozens of reporters, photographers, and television cameramen pushed and shoved, scribbling down every word Clifford spoke as flashbulbs popped.

Out of a white plastic pail he pulled two cannonballs, each about three inches in diameter, and held them up for everyone to see.

Then he held high above his head an x-ray of a piece of iron about three feet long and four or five inches wide.

"I'll say this," he began. "I don't expect everyone to agree with me. I'll stake it on whatever reputation I have, bad or good." The x-ray, he explained, showed the end of a heavy cutting sword. "Of course we know very little about the pirates. We do know that they were flamboyant."

He pointed to a dark circle in the x-ray at the tip of the sword.

"Without question, this is a coin. It's exactly three centimeters wide and that's the same width as a gold doubloon."

The coin was embedded in the tip of the sword.

"That to me suggests more than anything the spirit of what these pirates were about.

"I'm not going to ask anybody to agree with me. All I'm asking is for your help. We've got a highly concentrated wreck there, a highly concentrated scattering. We've dug in one small spot with the least amount of concentration that our magnetometer suggested. We're going to need as much time as possible. We're not planning on digging any new test pits. We're not planning on excavating. Those are the furthest things from our minds until we identify the perimeter of the wreck.

"If it is a pirate ship, and I'm saying that it is, then we have an incredibly rich find archaeologically."

And then, a shroud of silence settled over the *Whydah* expedition.

For the next two months, Clifford worked to line up a group of experts, headed by Michael Roberts, a marine archaeologist who had been director of the marine archaeology program at Harvard University's Peabody Museum, and including twenty-five other marine archaeologists and preservationists. He retained the Maritime Archaeological and Historical Research Institute, which took over the archaeological investigation of the wreck. "We realized that we really needed the best in archaeologists. The wreck warranted it." At the same time, a lab was set up to begin work on the preservation of the artifacts that had been recovered.

In September, Clifford and his team of archaeologists blasted out two more test pits, one close to the first, and the other where preliminary surveys seemed to indicate the presence of a section of the ship's hull. Shortly thereafter, the Board of Underwater Archeological Resources held a closed session to discuss security for the wreck. Leaving the meeting, Clifford's attorney told reporters that any who had been skeptical of the salvage operation should get ready "to eat crow." Asked when, he replied, "Soon."

It was not until early December that the veil of secrecy surrounding the diving operations was finally lifted.

In his first public comment since July, Barry Clifford reported that in the initial test pit, his divers had discovered a treasure hoard of over three thousand silver coins of the Spanish empire, including 2019 Mexican coins and 996 Peruvian coins, four gold coins, gold and silver jewelry, three cuff links, and a candlesnuffer, a collection of which clattered onto a table as Clifford emptied out a bag of pirate coins. "Imagine the sound of these down in the bilge of the ship when they counted them," Clifford remarked. In addition, mixed among this treasure were a flintlock pistol, a three-thousand-pound cannon, six cannonballs, 580 musket balls, and four trigger guards. From the two pits blasted out in September, the divers had recovered an encrusted mass of four cannon, an eight-foot-long anchor, silver coins, a silver bar, gold bars cut up for division among the pirates, gold dust, brass shoe buckles and cuff links, a sword sheath, and a mortar jar with the letter "W" scratched on its bottom.

The cannon were dated by archaeologists as having been made in the period 1680 to 1800. The flintlock pistol, with barrel and lockplate fashioned of brass inscribed with a decorative sea serpent, bore the gunsmith's mark of John Brooke, whose London workshop was in operation from 1703 to 1715. The trigger guards, the archaeologists concluded, could not have been made after 1720. And the 656 coins with legible dates were minted between 1638 and 1716.

"We have several million dollars in treasure," Clifford

noted. A single coin was valued at $40,000. He had yet to begin exploration of the areas where artifacts were thickly concentrated. "We're probably in the ballast, up toward the bow of the boat. If we dug seven and a half test pits a day it would take the next ten years to complete the excavation. They probably had ten tons of treasure on this thing. We have barely scratched the surface."

At last, Barry Clifford's expedition had located where the pirate ship had broken apart, but for many months he could do nothing about it. The 1985 diving season, which held so much promise, was delayed while Clifford waited to receive a permit from the Army Corps of Engineers, which regulated all work in navigable waters. Although as the summer sped by, Clifford assailed the "bureaucratic and laborious process" and "ivory tower archaeologists" who were holding back his project, he was sure "if we can get a month out there we'll bring up a tremendous amount of treasure." Through June, July, and August he waited, fairly bursting with the "enthusiasm anybody involved in a treasure hunt" would have. As soon as the permit is granted, Clifford reported, "We're in the water. We're sitting at the dock, ready to leave!"

Finally, on September 6, 1985, he received the permit from the Army Corps of Engineers that enabled him to begin bringing up the pirate treasure. That very day, though a brisk autumnal wind buffeted the *Vast Explorer*, his divers were in the water. Now, they knew just where to look. From the test pits, the divers brought up a dozen navigational tools, pewter eating utensils bearing a royal African seal, a swivel gun, a gold ring, a casket of East Indian jewels, and small gold bars with knife marks indicating the pirates had cut them to divide into shares. The divers suctioned gold into plastic bags from the brilliant layers of gold dust that ran through the wet sand "like chocolate through ripple ice cream." And the first several dives of the day brought up two thousand more silver coins dating from the 1600s and early 1700s. "Every dive we bring up hundreds of coins," Clifford remarked. "We haven't even started yet."

A month later, after $14 million of treasure had been salvaged, a several-hundred-pound hunk of clay and sand was hauled aboard the *Vast Explorer*. Embedded in the mass was an eighteen-inch bronze bell. Thick layers of incrustation and corrosion were chipped away. There, inscribed on the bell that had chimed the watches, were the magic words: "THE WHYDAH GALLY 1716."

Long before he had found the first Spanish coin protruding from the edge of the test pit, much earlier in the *Whydah* expedition, on those summer days when he had raced up the coast in his outboard for another day of diving the pale green waters off the Cape, Barry Clifford had found the legendary treasure.

"My life right now is a fantasy. What I mean is, how many people actually get to hunt for buried treasure in their lives?

"I'm not in this for the money. If I had all the money in the world, I'd pay to do this. We could have blown the whole thing off in a matter of hours and be flying around in Lear jets if we wanted to, but this means something to us.

"Every day there's something different. My mind is going three hundred miles an hour. I'm out on the edge, just like that wreck. I'm on the edge and I'm looking back at the rest of the country. I like that feeling. I never want to stop. Ever."

The treasure was there. There should never have been any doubt about that. Neither the wreckers nor centuries of tides and storms had found it or taken it away.

And the treasure would always be there for those who knew how to look, for as much a treasure as the bags of Spanish doubloons and silver pieces of eight and chests full of elephant-trunk ivory and coffers of rubies, is the story of young Captain Samuel Bellamy going upon the account, of the voyage and wreck of the *Whydah*, of Cyprian Southack's attempt to salvage the pirate hoard and Cotton Mather's efforts to save the pirates' souls, and of Maria Hallett, wandering the dunes of Cape Cod, waiting.

Captain Bellamy's beloved *Whydah* had finally been found, the only pirate ship ever to have been discovered. Two and a half centuries dropped away. The treasure, the plunder from the year-long pirate cruise on the Spanish Main, could now be divided.

A NOTE ON SOURCES

By the very nature of who they were and what they did, pirates
were shadowy figures who have long eluded the historian. It is
only because of the wreck of the *Whydah* on the shores of Cape
Cod and the resulting inquiries that there exists a remarkably
rich lode of contemporary materials about Captain Samuel
Bellamy and his crew. Each of these primary sources examines
the events from a different perspective; when these sources are
viewed together, as with the twist of the lens of a telescope, the
events that occurred over two and a half centuries ago come into
focus.

Captain Cyprian Southack was an inveterate letter writer and
journal keeper, and, although his efforts to salvage the treasure
of the *Whydah* were not among his proudest moments, he recorded every detail in letters to Governor Samuel Shute as well as
in his journal. These documents have been preserved in the
collections of the Massachusetts State Archives. Although his

spelling was atrocious and his rolling archaic script erratic at best, his records are an accurate report of the several weeks after the wreck that he spent in trying to recover the pirate gold. Chapter 5 is based on these records.

Issues of the *Boston News-Letter* for the years 1717 through 1718, preserved by the Massachusetts Historical Society, provide a contemporary account of the wreck and the trial of the pirates.

"Instructions to the LIVING from the Condition of the DEAD. A Brief Relation of REMARKABLES in the Shipwreck of above One Hundred PIRATES, Who were Cast away in the Ship *Whido*, on the Coast of New-England, April 26, 1717. And in the Death of Six, who after a Fair Trial at Boston, were Convicted & Condemned, Octob. 22. And Executed, Novemb. 15, 1717. With some Account of the Discourse had with them on the way to their Execution. And a SERMON preached on their Occasion" was written by the Reverend Cotton Mather right after the execution of the pirates. This pamphlet records Cotton Mather's conversations with the pirates, which I have incorporated in chapter 7. Within a month after the executions, his pamphlet was printed in Boston at the Sign of the Bible in Cornhill; no doubt the hasty publication was to satisfy Bostonians' curiosity about the strange band of storm-tossed pirates and their fates. Similarly, the Reverend Mr. Mather's sermon "WARNINGS to Them that Make Haste to be RICH," the moral of which was "He that getteth Riches and not by Right, Shall leave them in the midst of his Days, and at his End Shall be a Fool" was delivered on December 8, 1717, and immediately published to show his congregation of the Second North Church and the people of Boston the meaning of this "very black Tragedy." Additional reflections of Cotton Mather on the events surrounding the wreck, the trial, and the execution of the pirates are contained in his Diaries.

A year after the wreck of the *Whydah* — on May 22, 1718, to be exact — Governor Shute appointed "Bartholomew Green to

Print the Trials of Simon Van Vorst, John Brown, Thomas
Baker, Hendrick Quintor, Peter Cornelius Hoof, John Shuan,
Thomas South, and Thomas Davis, To be Sold by John Edwards,
Bookseller in King Street, Boston; And that no other Person
presume to Print the same." Soon thereafter, on a table in a small
shop on King Street appeared the pamphlet "The TRIALS of
Eight Persons Indited for Piracy &c. Of who Two were acquitted,
and the rest found Guilty. At a Judiciary Court of Admiralty
Assembled and Held in Boston within His Majesty's Province
of the Massachusetts-Bay in New-England, on the 18th of
October 1717. and by several Adjournments continued on the
30th. Pursuant to His Majesty's Commission and Instructions,
founded on the Act of Parliament Made in the 11th. & 12th of
King William IIId. Intituled, An Act for the more effectual
Suppression of Piracy. With an APPENDIX, Containing the
Substance of their Confessions given before His Excellency the
Governour, when they were first brought to Boston, and committed to Gaol." This pamphlet contains both some summaries
and some verbatim transcripts of the trial of the pirates, which I
relied on in chapter 6, as well as transcripts of their confessions
when they first arrived in Boston. Additional affidavits and depo-
sitions of sailors who had encountered the pirates are contained
in the Suffolk, Massachusetts, Court Files. All of those documents
form the basis of the story of Captain Bellamy's career as a pirate,
which I have retold in chapters 2 through 4.

The chapter about Captain Bellamy in Daniel Defoe's book
*A General History of the Robberies and Murders of the Most
Notorious Pirates*, published in London in 1724, seven years after
the wreck of the *Whydah*, was probably based on Defoe's conversations with someone who had been directly involved in the
events, most likely a captive aboard Captain Paulsgrave Williams's
Mary Anne. To the extent that Defoe's account is plausible within
the context of other contemporary sources, I have relied on it in
this book. I have drawn my account of the storm off the coast of

Virginia, the play "The Royal Pirate," and Captain Bellamy's meeting with Captain Beer in chapter 3 from Defoe's history.

I am grateful to the staffs of the Massachusetts Historical Society, the Colonial Society of Massachusetts, the Massachusetts State Archives, the American Antiquarian Society, the Library of Congress, the Houghton Library of Harvard University, the Chatham (Massachusetts) Library, and the Summit (New Jersey) Free Public Library for their continuing assistance in making these documents and additional resources available to me.

The following is a selection of other sources that have been useful in the preparation of this book:

Andrews, Kenneth R. The *Spanish Caribbean*. New Haven: Yale University Press, 1978.

Bangs, Mary Rogers. *Old Cape Cod*. Boston: Houghton Mifflin Company, 1931.

Barnes, V. F. "The Rise of William Phips," in *New England Quarterly*, vol. 1, no. 280 (July 1928).

Botting, Douglas. *The Pirates*. Alexandria, Virginia: Time-Life Books, 1978.

Brigham, Albert Perry. *Cape Cod and the Old Colony*. New York: Grosset & Dunlap, 1920.

Burgess, Robert E. *Sinkings, Salvages and Shipwrecks*. New York: American Heritage Press, 1970.

Celebrated Trials and Remarkable Cases of Criminal Jurisprudence from the Earliest Records to the Year 1825, vol. 3. London: Knight and Lacey, 1825.

Chamberlain, Barbara Blau. "Cape Cod," in *Natural History*, vol. 76, no. 5 (May 1967).

———. *These Fragile Outposts*. New York: The Natural History Press, 1964.

Corbett, Scott. *Cape Cod's Way*. New York: Thomas Y. Crowell Company, 1954.

Crosby, Katherine. *Blue-Water Men and Other Cape Codders*. New York: Macmillan Company, 1946.

Daley, Robert. *Treasure*. New York: Random House, 1977.

Dalton, J. W. *The Life Savers of Cape Cod*. Boston: Barta Press, 1902.

Dethlefsen, Edwin. *Whidah: Cape Cod's Mystery Treasure Ship*. Woodstock, Vermont: Seafarers Heritage Library, 1984.

Dictionary of American Biography. New York: Charles Scribner's Sons, 1934.

Digges, Jeremiah. *Cape Cod Pilot*. New York: Viking Press, 1937.

Dodson, James. "Not the Best of Times for Barry Clifford," in *Yankee*, vol. 48, no. 5 (March 1984).

Dow, George Francis, and John Henry Edmonds. *The Pirates of the New England Coast*. Salem, Massachusetts: Marine Research Society, 1923.

Edmonds, John. "By Boat Across the Cape: Channel Formerly Existed Through Which the Atlantic Could Be Reached from Barnstable Bay — How It Was Used in 1717 by Capt. Southack, Who Buried the Dead from the Wrecked Pirate Ship Whido," in *Boston Sunday Globe* (November 13, 1904).

"An Exact and Perfect Relation of the Arrival of the Ship the JAMES and MARY Captain PHIPPS Commander, With 200000 l. in Gold and Silver, taken up in nine Fathom Water from the bottom of the Sea, being a Suppos'd Wreck of a Spanish Galion, Cast-away above 43 years ago among the Bahama Islands, as it was taken from the aforesaid Captain, now riding in Graves-end Road," broadside printed in London in June 1687, from the collection of the Massachusetts Historical Society.

Exquemelin, A. O. *The Buccaneers of America*. London: Folio Society, 1969.

Freeman, Frederick. *History of Cape Cod*. Boston: printed for the author, 1858.

George, Robert H. "The Treasure Trove of William Phips," in *New England Quarterly*, vol. 5, no. 300 (June 1933).

Jameson, J. F. *Privateering and Piracy*. New York: Macmillan Company, 1923.

Johnson, Merle (compiler). *Howard Pyle's Book of Pirates*. New York: Harper and Brothers, 1921.

Karraker, Cyrus H. *The Hispaniola Treasure*. Philadelphia: University of Pennsylvania Press, 1934.

Kittredge, Henry C. *Cape Cod: Its People and Their History*. Boston: Houghton Mifflin, 1968.

———. *Mooncussers of Cape Cod*. Boston: Houghton Mifflin, 1937.

Levin, David. *Cotton Mather: The Young Life of the Lord's Remembrancer*. Cambridge: Harvard University Press, 1978.

Marx, Robert F. *The Treasure Fleets of the Spanish Main*. New York: World Publishing, 1968.

Mather, Cotton. *Pietas in Patriam*. London: publisher unknown, 1697.

Middlekauft, Robert. *The Mathers: Three Generations of Puritan Intellectuals, 1596–1728*. New York: Random House, 1971.

"Monomoy," in *Harpers New Monthly Magazine* (February 1864).

Morison, Samuel Eliot. *The European Discovery of America: The Southern Voyages* (New York: Oxford University Press, 1974).

Osgood, Herbert L. *The American Colonies in the Eighteenth Century*. New York: Columbia University Press, 1924.

Otis, Amos. "An Account of the Discovery of an Ancient Ship on the Eastern Shore of Cape Cod," in *The New England Historical and Genealogical Register for the Year 1864*, vol. 18 (1864), pp. 37 ff.

Parry, J. H. *Romance of the Sea*. Washington, D.C.: National Geographic Book Service, 1981.

Peterson, Mendel. *The Funnel of Gold*. New York: Little, Brown, 1975.

Putnam, Robert. *Early Sea Charts*. New York: Abbeville Press, 1983.

Quinn, William P. *Shipwrecks Around Cape Cod*. Farmington, Maine: Knowlton & McLeary Company, 1973.

Reynard, Elizabeth. *The Narrow Land*. Boston: Houghton Mifflin Company, 1962.

Rich, Earle. *More Cape Cod Echoes*. Orleans, Massachusetts: Salt Meadow Publishers, 1978.

Richman, Irving Berdine. *The Spanish Conquerors: A Chronicle of the Dawn of Empire Overseas*. New Haven: Yale University Press, 1921.

Ryan, Michael. "Barry Clifford's Zany Crew — Including JFK Jr. — Prove that 'Way Down Deep, They're Golddiggers," in *People* magazine (August 22, 1983).

Seafaring in Colonial Massachusetts. Boston: Colonial Society of Massachusetts, 1980.

Silverman, Kenneth. *The Life and Times of Cotton Mather*. New York: Harper & Row, 1984.

Small, Isaac M. *Shipwrecks on Cape Cod*. Chatham, Massachusetts: Chatham Press, Inc., 1967.

Snelgrave, Captain William. *A New Account of Some Parts of Guinea and the Slave-Trade*. London: Frank Cass & Co. Ltd., 1971.

Snow, Edward Rowe. *Great Storms and Famous Shipwrecks of the New England Coast*. Boston: Yankee Publishing Company, 1943.

———. *True Tales of Buried Treasure*. New York: Dodd, Mead & Company, 1960.

Thoreau, Henry David. *Cape Cod*. New York: Thomas Y. Crowell Company, 1961.

White, David Fairbank. "How the Sea Gave Up a $400 Million Pirate Treasure," in *Parade* magazine (January 27, 1985).

Whitman, Levi. "A Topographical Description of Wellfleet in the County of Barnstable," in *Collections of the Massachusetts Historical Society for the Year 1794*, vol. 3, p. 117.

Wood, Peter. *The Spanish Main*. Alexandria, Virginia: Time-Life Books, 1979.